Using Multicultural Literature

OVERCOMING DIFFICULTIES

Primary

Editor:
Dona Herweck Rice

Editorial Director:
Sharon Coan, M.S. Ed.

Art Direction:
Elayne Roberts

Cover Artist:
Neena Chawla

Imaging:
Rick Chacón

Publishers:
Rachelle Cracchiolo, M.S. Ed.
Mary Dupuy Smith, M.S. Ed.

Author:
Linda Burrell Hill

Illustrators:
Sue Fullam and Barb Lorseyedi

Teacher Created Materials, Inc.
P.O. Box 1040
Huntington Beach, Ca 92647
©1994 Teacher Created Materials, Inc.
Made in U.S.A.

ISBN #1-55734-665-8

Table of Contents

Introduction/Overview **4**

Crow Boy by Taro Yashima (Puffin, 1976)
(Available in Canada, UK & AUS: Penguin, Ltd.)

Summing It Up *and* **Getting to Know the Author and Illustrator** **5**

Getting Started **6**
>   Facts About Japan

People Are People **8**
>   Familiar Feelings; Chibi and You; Differences

Socializing Skills Project: Teasing **12**
>   Discussion Pictures; Dealing With Teasing

Getting from Here to There **16**
>   Cardinal Directions; L.A.'s Little Tokyo; Japan and the U.S.A.; Japanese Exports; Finding
>   America in Japan

Experiencing the Culture **22**
>   Bookmark Proverbs; Kanji; Daruma; Japanese Recipes; Games from Japan; Haiku; Cherry
>   Blossom Art

Community Ties **31**
>   Flag Patterns; Sights of Our Town; Sounds of Our Town; Profile on Kristi Yamaguchi; Kristi
>   Crossword; Map Kristi's Day; Whose Shoe?

The Legend of the Indian Paintbrush by Tomie dePaola (Macmillan, 1988)
(Available in Canada: BeJo Sales; UK & AUS: Baker & Taylor Int.)

Summing It Up *and* **Getting to Know the Author and Illustrator** **40**

Getting Started **41**

People Are People **43**
>   I Can't/I Can; Meet Little; Fold Book; Words That Won't Quit

Socializing Skills Project: Keeping a Promise **48**
>   How Would You Feel?; A Guide to Making Promises; A Promise You Can Keep

Getting from Here to There **52**
>   Buffalo Hunt; A Moving Village

Experiencing the Culture **55**
>   Living in a Tepee; Reservation Life; Build a House; Shared Values; Plains Indian Games;
>   Pop-Up Name Tag; Contribution Puzzle; Match the Dresses; Silent Talking; Indian Recipes;
>   Artistic Expressions; Parfleche; Buffalo Game; Fair Trade

Community Ties **75**
>   Native Americans in My Community

Table of Contents *(cont.)*

Amazing Grace by Mary Hoffman (Dial, 1991)
(Available in Canada, UK & AUS: Penguin Books)

Summing It Up *and* Getting to Know the Author and Illustrator 77

Getting Started 78

People Are People 80

Grace's Feelings; Real or Make-Believe?; Great People from the Past

Socializing Skills Project: Breaking Down Stereotypes 84

Breaking Down Stereotypes; Unscrambling Stereotypes; A Dream for Me!

Getting from Here to There 88

Putting It All Together; Using Symbols; Big Deals; Queen's Park, Savannah

Experiencing the Culture 94

Carnival Music; Kente Cloth and Adinkra; Color the Kente Cloth; Day Names; _____'s Book of Proverbs; African-American Recipes; Games from Africa and Trinidad; Traveling with Grace Game

Community Ties 106

Discovery Day Survey for Parents; Flags of Trinidad, Ghana, and the United States; People at Work in Trinidad and Ghana

Nessa's Fish by Nancy Luenn (Atheneum, 1990)
(Available in Canada, UK & AUS: Macmillan)

Summing It Up *and* Getting to Know the Author and Illustrator 111

Getting Started 112

Go Away!; I Can Be Scary

People Are People 116

Socializing Skills Project: Bravery 117

Foolish or Brave?; Brave Enough; Bravery Bulletin Boards; Award of Bravery

Getting from Here to There 123

The Poles; Seasons in the Arctic and at Home; Complete the Map

Experiencing the Culture 128

Arctic Transportation; Inuit Games; Inuktitut: The Inuit Language; Inuit Recipes; Make Your Own Mittens; Make Your Own Mukluks; What Keeps You Warm?; The Snowy Owl

Community Ties 138

What I Need to Know About Me; When You Are Lost

Bibliography 141

Answer Key 142-144

Introduction/Overview

The basic purpose of multicultural education is to prepare students to live harmoniously in a multi-ethnic society. Our nation is rooted in cultures from around the world. Although every culture is not represented in all classrooms, our nation certainly represents the diversity that exists in the world. The series entitled *Using Multicultural Literature* is designed to be used in all classrooms to teach students skills needed to live, work, and socialize in a culturally pluralistic society. The goals of this book are these:

1. To promote historical, geographic, cultural, and ethnic literacy.
2. To build knowledge of how people of various cultures live and what they value.
3. To develop respect for the human dignity of all people and the social responsibility needed in a multi-ethnic society.
4. To help students develop a positive attitude toward themselves and their cultural identities.

Teachers can use this book to supplement their social studies curriculum. Each unit is based on a piece of children's literature that presents a culture in a non-stereotypical, positive arena. The seven disciplines of social studies (history, geography, economics, anthropology, sociology, philosophy, and psychology) are woven into each unit.

Summing It Up gives a synopsis of the reading selection.

Getting to Know the Author and Illustrator presents a brief author biography and a simple description of the illustrator's style.

Getting Started brings students into the literature and prepares them to learn more about the culture involved.

People Are People draws a connection between the protagonist and the students by discussing the basic human characteristics present in all cultures.

The Socializing Skills Project teaches a social responsibility that is needed in an ethical society.

Getting from Here to There teaches geography skills such as mapping and graphing.

Experiencing the Culture increases understanding of the given culture through activities involving values, music, food, clothing, and more.

Community Ties connects the culture from the literature to the students' cultures through exposure to the diversity within their own society.

Crow Boy: Summing It Up

A small, shy Japanese boy named Chibi ("tiny boy") is rather different from the other children in school. On the first day of classes, he hides beneath the building. Because he is afraid of the teacher and the other children, he becomes a loner and is teased by his classmates. He is known as a lazy class clown, daydreaming instead of concentrating on his lessons.

In the sixth grade, Chibi's new teacher takes the time to get to know him, and the teacher discovers many of Chibi's hidden talents. For example, the boy understands a great deal about nature, and he has a particular understanding about crows. At the end-of-the-year talent show, Chibi surprises everyone with an impressive array of crow imitations. In so doing, he creates an image of the mountain where he has grown up. Through his talent and his willingness to share something of himself, Chibi gains respect and acceptance. His new nickname—a term of endearment—is Crow Boy.

Getting to Know the Author and Illustrator

Taro Yashima is the pen name for Jun Atusushi Twamatsu. Mr. Twamatsu was born in Kagoshima, Japan. In 1939, he came to the United States. He began writing and illustrating children's books to help his own daughter understand his childhood in Japan. *The New Sun* is his autobiography.

Mr. Twamatsu has directed the Yashima Art Institute in Washington, D.C., and his artwork has been exhibited throughout the country. *Crow Boy* is a Caldecott Honor Book, an award given for excellent achievement in illustration. His artwork in *Crow Boy* captures the simplicity and gaiety of life in Japan. Using pastel and ink strokes, he is able to create illustrations which draw the reader into the story. Yashima uses an impressionistic style to highlight the beauty of the country.

Getting Started

1. **Japanese American History:** Share with the students the following information about the history of the Japanese in America.

   In the 1890's, the Japanese settled in Hawaii and worked on sugarcane plantations. In 1898, when the United States annexed Hawaii, many Japanese moved to the mainland. Most settled on the west coast. By 1900, about 12,600 had moved to the United States. During the first two decades of the 20th century, 214,000 Japanese (only 30,000 of whom were women) had immigrated to the United States.

   From 1907 to 1948, anti-Japanese bills were introduced in every session of the California legislature. Asians were barred from U.S. citizenship. A 1913 California law banned purchase of land by aliens. In 1926, the U.S. Immigration Act was passed, which prohibited the Japanese from immigration to the United States.

   On February 19, 1942, President Franklin D. Roosevelt signed Executive Order 9066 which led to the internment of Japanese Americans. Japanese Americans living on the west coast were moved to ten concentration camps in various remote areas of the United States. The camps were located in Arizona, Arkansas, California, Colorado, Idaho, Utah, and Wyoming. Many Japanese Americans joined the military during the war in dramatic proof of their loyalty. The 100/442nd regimental combat team was the most decorated unit for its size and length of service. More than 18,000 individual citations for bravery were awarded to the 100/442nd.

   In 1945, when the government began closing down the camps, many Japanese Americans were free to return to their homes. Unfortunately, most of their possessions and property were gone. Banks had sold property due to defaulted loans, and some personal property placed in storage was stolen. The Japanese Americans were forced to start over again.

   In March of 1946, the last concentration camp closed. In 1952, the California alien laws were repealed, and Congress granted citizenship to Japanese immigrants. Once again, despite their many harrowing experiences, the Japanese began immigrating to the United States.

2. **Drawing Japan:** Provide each child with a blank piece of paper and ask him/her to draw a picture of Japan. Allow the children to draw a scene, person, map, or anything else they feel will represent Japan. Encourage them to draw as much detail as possible. Save these pictures.

   At the end of the unit, have the children do this assignment again. When comparing the pre and post instruction pictures, look for accuracy of details, relationships, and organizational structures that show evidence of growth in knowledge.

3. **Facts About Japan:** Share the information from page 7 with the students. Use it for project reports, quizzes, or discussion about the country.

Facts About Japan

Official Name: Nippon ("Source of the Sun")

Capital: Tokyo

National Anthem: *"Kimigayo"* ("The Reign of Our Emperor")

Land Area: 145,870 square miles (377,801 km²)

Coastline: 5,857 miles (9,426 km)

Four Major Islands: Hokkaido, Honshu, Kyushu, and Shikoku (There are many smaller islands.)

Highest Point: Mt. Fuji—12,388 feet (3,776 m)

Lowest Point: sea level

Population: over 123 million (1991)

Official Language: Japanese

Government: constitutional monarchy

Emperor: Akihito

Labor Distribution: commerce and service, 50%; manufacturing, 24%; construction, 10%; agriculture and fishing, 10%; government and public services, 6%

Basic Form of Money: yen

National Flag: red circle (sun) on a white background

National Holidays: Emperor's birthday (April 29), New Year's Day (January 1), Constitution Day (May 3), Doll Festival or Girl's Day (March 3), Children's Day or Boy's Day (May 5)

Traditional Arts and Customs: *kabuki* (classical play that combines singing, acting, and dancing), *no* (poetic treatment of history and legends in a play form), *chano-yu* (tea ceremony), and *ikebana* (flower arrangement)

Major Religions: Shinto, Buddhism, and Christianity

Clothing: *kimono* (worn only on special occasions), *surippa* (slippers worn inside the house instead of shoes), *geta* (wooden clogs), and *zori* (flat sandals)

Sports: baseball (most popular), *sumo* wrestling, and *kendo*

People Are People

The purpose of these lessons is to teach students that they may have the same feelings as Crow Boy, and like Crow Boy, their feelings can change.

1. **Crow Boy's Feelings:** After reading the book to the class, discuss Crow Boy's feelings. You might have students brainstorm for what those feelings are. (Make sure that loneliness and pride are included in the discussion.) Write the brainstormed feelings on butcher paper and save this paper as a reminder about feelings. You might take it a step further to share times when the students may have felt just as Crow Boy does in various parts of the story.

2. **Familiar Feelings:** Point out that Crow Boy's feelings change during the book. Ask the children how they felt on the first day of school and how their feelings have changed. Give each student a copy of page 9. This worksheet can be completed independently after the directions have been read and discussed. Students will need crayons and a pencil to do the work.

3. **Changing Names:** Explain to the class that in the beginning of the book, the main character is referred to as Chibi, but at the end of the story he is called Crow Boy. Ask the class why they think this change occurs. The students should realize that as the feelings of the characters change, the main character's name changes.

4. **Chibi and You:** Give each student a copy of page 10. This exercise should be done as a whole-group activity. To help students who are unfamiliar with completing a check-off sheet, you may want to make an overhead master.

5. **Differences:** Ask the students why Chibi is teased. Write their responses on the board. Sum up all the responses in the following statement: "The children tease Chibi because he is different."

   Ask the students if they are exactly like anyone else in the class. Guide them to the conclusion that we are all different. Explain that being different is no reason to tease.

   For page 11, have each child choose a classmate. Everyone will write about how a classmate is different from him or her. Refer to their responses from "Chibi and You" (page 10). On the chalkboard, you may want to brainstorm a word bank for each question. The first set of blanks may be filled with the two students' names or with physical descriptions (like *short* and *tall*).

Name_____

Familiar Feelings

Directions: Draw a picture in each box. Write a sentence below each that tells how you and Chibi feel in the picture. Then, answer the questions at the bottom of the page.

Chibi's First Day at School   Your First Day at School

_____   _____

_____   _____

1. How would you feel if other children teased you?

    _____

2. How do you think Chibi feels when he is teased?

    _____

3. Why do the children tease Chibi?

    _____

Name_____

Chibi and You

Directions: Compare yourself to Chibi by putting a check to the left of the words that have at any time been true for you and to the right of the words that have at any time been true for Chibi.

Me		Chibi
_____	Feels bored at school.	_____
_____	Teases others.	_____
_____	Walks to school.	_____
_____	Brings lunch to school.	_____
_____	Has perfect attendance.	_____
_____	Plays during recess.	_____
_____	Has friends.	_____
_____	Listens to the teacher.	_____
_____	Is helpful at home.	_____
_____	Understands nature.	_____

Name_____

Differences

Directions: Fill in the blanks, and then draw pictures that go with what you wrote.

My name is _____, and my friend's name is_____.

I like to _____, but my friend likes to _____.

I am good at _____, and my friend is good at _____.

As you can see, though we are
different, we can still be friends.

Socializing Skills Projects: Teasing

1. **Preparing for the Lesson:** Copy and color pages 13 and 14. (Enlarge them if possible.) Mount each on a piece of construction paper so that they may be posted in the classroom.

2. **Discussion:** Begin the lesson by having the students share their responses about teasing from the exercise on page 9. Explain to the children that they are going to learn why they should not tease.

3. **Discussion Pictures:** Tell the children that although Chibi never cries or becomes angry when he is teased, his feelings are still hurt. Show the class the picture entitled "Teasing Hurts Feelings" (page 13). Ask the children how it feels to be teased. Explain that when a person is teased, it is hard for that person to feel good about him or herself. Discuss some of the ways that Chibi acts out because his feelings are hurt. Then, have each student color his/her own copy of the page.

   Next, ask the children if they think Chibi would like to be friends with the children who are teasing him. Then, show them the picture entitled "You Can't Make a Friend by Teasing Him or Her" (page 13). Discuss why it is difficult to be friends with a person who teases. Make sure they realize that nobody likes to be teased. Explain that a person risks losing friends if that person teases. Then, have the students color their own copy of the page.

   Now, ask the children to think of the qualities a nice person has. Listen to them, and then show them the picture entitled "Nice People Don't Tease" (page 14). Explain that nice people do not like to hurt others, but they do like to make friends. If you tease, you are not being nice. Conclude this section of the discussion by coloring individual copies of this picture.

   Finally, ask the class what the consequences at home and at school are for teasing another person. Show the picture entitled "Teasing Can Get You in Trouble" (page 14). Explain that teasing does not solve problems, but many times it can create them. Allow the children to share some of the problems that they think teasing can cause. Then, have each child color a copy of the picture.

   Give each student a folded piece of construction paper to use as a cover for a book entitled "Why We Don't Tease." They can write the title of the book on the cover and then decorate it. The four pictures they colored will be the inside pages. When the pages are finished, staple the book together or punch holes and tie the pages together with yarn.

4. **Dealing With Teasing:** Teach the children the following rule: "If you can't say something nice, then don't say anything at all." Have them copy this rule onto a piece of paper and draw a picture to go with it. Then, in small groups, have the children share their pictures. Ask them to discuss what they do when somebody teases them. Have a spokesperson from the group report to the class about the group's discussion.

   Distribute page 15 to each student. Discuss the three strategies for dealing with teasing that are provided on the page. After reading each solution, have each child draw a picture of how he/she would use it. Discuss.

Discussion Pictures

Teasing Hurts Feelings.

You Can't Make a Friend by Teasing Him or Her.

Discussion Pictures *(cont.)*

Nice People Don't Tease.

Teasing Can Get You in Trouble.

Name_____

Dealing With Teasing

Ignore teasing.

Walk away.

Play with people who do not tease.

Getting from Here to There

1. **Cardinal Directions:** Display a large map of the United States and ask the children how people know which way to hold the map when they are looking at it. After listening to their ideas, tell them that the north side of the map is always at the top of the page.

   Ask the children if they know of any other cardinal directions. After the three remaining directions (south, east, and west) have been given, divide the class into cooperative groups of four. Give each group the four cardinal direction cards found on page 17. Allow each student to choose a card.

   The class will then stand, and the students holding the north card will face the northern part of the classroom. The students holding the south card will then stand back-to-back with the north-facing students. East will take his/her place, and west will follow.

   Next, have each child hand his/her card to the person on his/her left. When everybody has a new card, have the children face the new direction. This game can be repeated a few times until all the children understand the four cardinal directions. You can also have the children keep passing the cards while you play music, and when the music stops, each child will have to resume a new position in the classroom.

2. **L.A.'s Little Tokyo:** Give each child a copy of page 18. Tell them that it is a map of a Japanese-American business community located in Los Angeles, CA. Explain that the small pictures on the map are called symbols and that symbols represent things. The box in the bottom corner tells what the symbols represent.

   Have the students locate the cardinal directions on the map. The questions at the bottom can be answered in a class discussion.

3. **Japan and the U.S.A.:** Page 19 is a map of Japan and the west coast of the United States. The students can demonstrate what they have learned about directions by filling in the blanks pertaining to the map. Review the words in the word bank, and then complete the questions.

4. **Japanese Exports:** Give each student a copy of page 20. Explain that this chart includes both symbols and words. Ask the children if they can determine what each symbol represents.

   The chart shows approximately how much of each product (in dollars) is sent to America from Japan per year. The students will use the chart to answer the questions.

5. **Finding America in Japan:** Explain that Japan and the United States import and export many of their products to one another. They also exchange a number of ideas, behaviors, and styles. The picture on page 21 shows many things in Japan that come from America. Have the students locate and circle (or list) as many of them as they can.

Cardinal Directions

East

North

West

South

Name_____

L.A.'s Little Tokyo

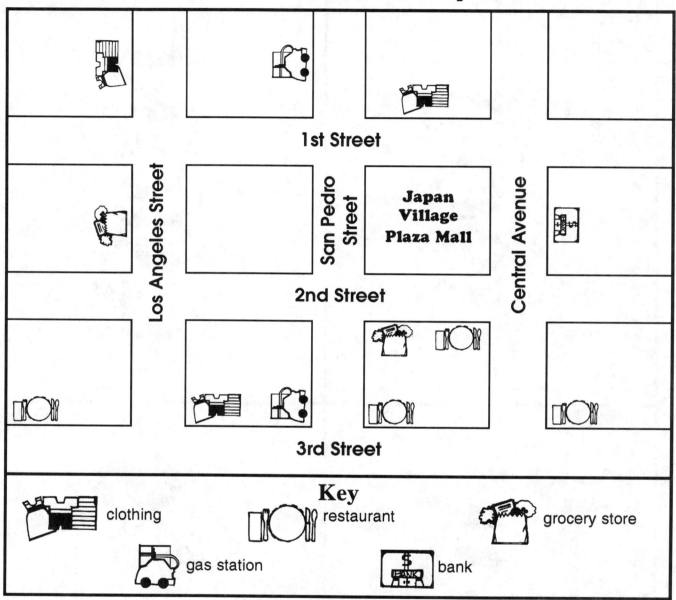

Directions: Use the map to answer the questions.

1. How many restaurants are on 3rd Street? _____

2. Is there a grocery store on Los Angeles Street? _____

3. What business is north of the mall? _____

4. How many gas stations are on San Pedro Street? _____

5. On what street is the bank? _____

Name_____

Japan and the U.S.A.

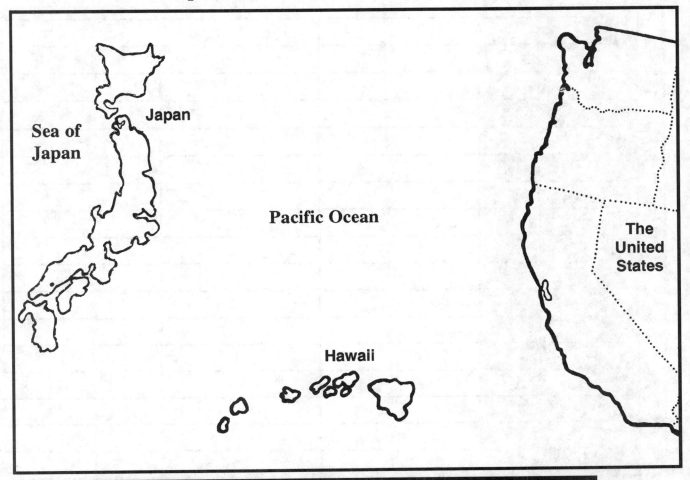

Sea of
Japan

Japan

Pacific Ocean

The
United
States

Hawaii

Word Bank

east	plane	west
Pacific Ocean	boat	Sea of Japan
	islands	

Directions: Fill in the statements below with words from the word bank.

1. To get to Japan from the U.S.A., you can travel by _____ or _____.

2. Japan is _____ of the United States.

3. The _____ is between the two nations.

4. Japan and the state of Hawaii are both _____.

5. The United States is _____ of Japan.

6. The _____ is west of Japan.

Name_____

Japanese Exports

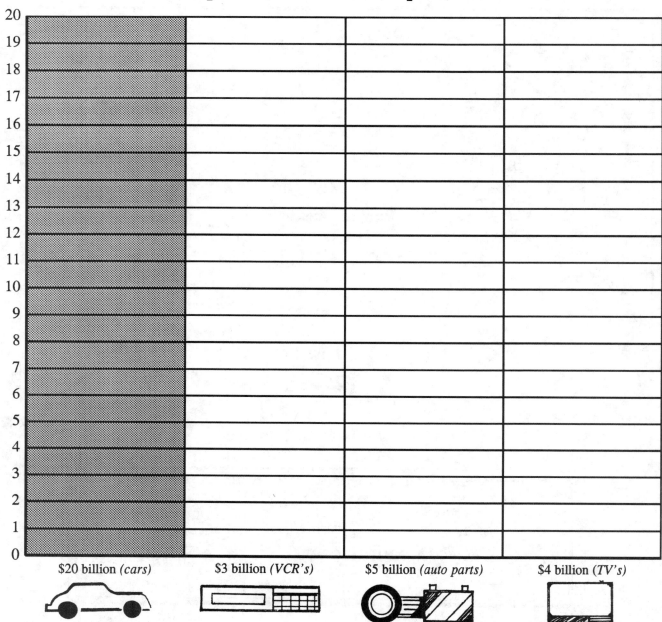

Directions: Color in the bars on this graph to show how many billion dollars of products were exported from Japan to the United States in a recent year. The first one has been done for you. Then, answer the questions below.

1. Which export made the most money? _____

2. Which export made the least money? _____

3. Which export made more money than TV's but less money than cars?

_____

Name_____

Finding America in Japan

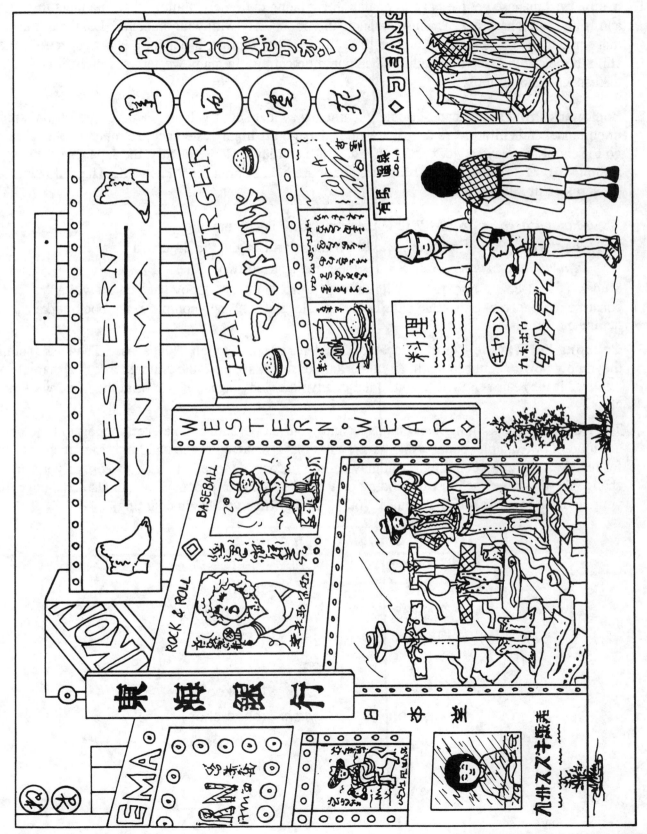

Experiencing the Culture

1. **Manners:** Japanese people have a reputation for being extremely polite. Their manners to guests and friends are charming. Discuss manners in your society with your students. Let them know that some manners vary depending on the culture. For example, in Japan, it is disrespectful for a child to look at the face of an adult when communicating. In many western societies, it is disrespectful not to look.

2. **Bookmark Proverbs:** Japanese society maintains a clear set of values. Families are of the utmost importance, and children are deeply loved. Education is highly esteemed, so much so that children go to school five days a week and half a day on Saturday. (Consequently, the Japanese population is almost 100% literate.) Friendship and honor are held in high regard as well. The following proverbs exhibit these values.

   Manabazareba shirazu - Without learning there is no knowing.

   Kokoro tadashi keriba koto tadashi - If the heart is right, the deed will be right.

   Yujo wa ittai doshin - Friendship is the same heart in two bodies.

   Students can decorate bookmarks with these proverbs on them. Copy page 24 on white construction paper, and then have the students color them. When complete, the bookmarks can be laminated for durability.

3. **Counting the Ways to Count:** Teach your students to count to ten in Japanese. Then ask them if they know how to count to ten in any other language. Also, have the children ask their parents or relatives if they know how to count to ten in any other languages. Share what they find with the class.

   To incorporate counting in other languages into your daily routine, take every opportunity to count out loud. For example, count while papers or books are passed to the children. Line the class up for recess or lunch by counting. You may choose to focus on one language a week, or you can change the language each day depending on the ability of your group. You can also challenge your students to guess which language you are using when you begin counting.

Counting in Japanese

one	*itchi*	(ee-chee)
two	*ni*	(nee)
three	*san*	(sahn)
four	*shi*	(shee)
five	*go*	(goh)
six	*roku*	(roh-koo)
seven	*shishi*	(shee-chee)
eight	*hachi*	(hah-chee)
nine	*ku*	(koo)
ten	*ju*	(joo)

Experiencing the Culture *(cont.)*

4. **Kanji:** There are three ways of writing used by the Japanese. They are as follows:

    a. Using the same letters as in the English alphabet.

    b. Using *Kana* (or *Katakana*), symbols that stand for a sound in much the same way a letter or group of letters in the English alphabet stands for a particular sound. There are one hundred Kana.

    c. Using *Hiragana,* which was developed from the cursive writing of Kanji.

    Kanji are symbols that represent words. They were adopted by the Japanese thousands of years ago, and there are over 1,800 that fully literate people must remember. On page 25, you will find some simple Kanji that students may enjoy writing.

5. **Daruma:** This is a good luck symbol in Japan, representing the spirit of courage and determination. It is named after a Buddhist monk who meditated for nine years. He sat so still that he lost the use of his legs and arms.

    A saying goes with the daruma: "Seven times you may fall, but eight times you will rise up again." A daruma is used when a person wants something good to happen to him/her or when a person is trying to accomplish a goal.

    Use the pattern on page 26 to make a daruma. Run off two for each student on heavy construction paper or tagboard. Cut the patterns out and tape or staple the daruma at the top. The students may decorate the daruma, but they cannot color in the eyes. Have the students think of something that they want to accomplish by a specific date. The goal can be as simple as remembering to bring lunch money for an entire week or getting all of their math work finished on time. Then they may color in one eye of their daruma. When their goal has been accomplished, they may color in the other eye.

6. **Japanese Recipes**: The delicious recipes found on page 27 may be made at school or at home. The students may also learn the art of *Kuai-zi,* or using chopsticks. Follow these directions:

    a. Place one chopstick in the hand, laying the stick between the thumb and index finger. This chopstick will not move.

    b. Use your thumb, index finger, and two middle fingers to hold the second chopstick. This chopstick will move to pick up the food.

    c. Keep the bottom points of the chopstick even. To pick up the food, move the second chopstick to pinch the food against the first. Enjoy!

7. **Games from Japan:** Students will have an opportunity to see what Japanese and Americans have in common when playing the games described on page 28.

8. **Haiku:** Use page 29 to create original *haiku,* a very structured poem that usually refers to nature or seasons.

9. **Cherry Blossom Art:** The Japanese have a deep love of nature, and they celebrate its beauty. In early spring, they welcome the blooming of the cherry blossoms with a festival. There is a great deal of singing and dancing. See the bibliography for "The Cherry Blossom Song" source. Sing it as you make the art project on page 30.

Bookmark Proverbs

Manabazareba shirazu.

Without learning there is no knowing.

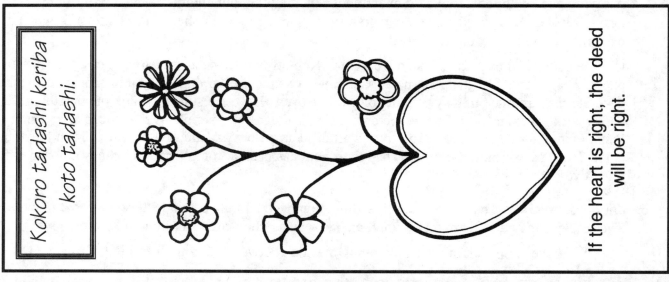

Kokoro tadashi keriba koto tadashi.

If the heart is right, the deed will be right.

Yujo wa ittai doshin.

Friendship is the same heart in two bodies.

Name_____

Kanji

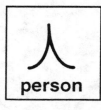  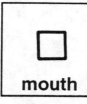   

Directions: Write the Kanji characters from above the line in the correct boxes below.

1. Chibi is a special

2. Chibi lives over the

3. He leaves for school when the   is rising .

4. With his   he listens to the crows.

5. With his   he makes crow sounds.

6. He returns home before the   rises in the sky.

Daruma

Japanese Recipes

Oriental Salad

This recipe is easy and will require minimal preparation time by the teacher. It can be prepared in small cooperative groups.

Ingredients:

- 3 slices mandarin orange
- 3 chunks pineapple
- ½ apple thinly sliced
- ½ teaspoon (3 mL) soy nuts
- 1 forkful of bean sprouts

Directions: Stir to mix. Eat with chopsticks. Serves one.

Japanese Tempura

This recipe is more difficult. It is best to have adult helpers when preparing it.

Ingredients:

- 1 egg
- 3 tbsp. (45 mL) flour
- ⅛ tbsp. (2 mL) salt
- 1 tbsp. water (15 mL)
- 1 carrot
- 1 small onion
- ½ cup (125 mL) parsley sprigs
- ½ cup (125 mL) oil
- soy sauce

Directions: To prepare the batter, beat the egg in a bowl. Add the flour, salt, and water. Mix until smooth.

To prepare the vegetables, cut two 2-inch (5 cm) pieces from the carrot, cut again in half lengthwise, slice thin, and then cut into matchstick pieces. Arrange in clusters, three to four carrot sticks together. Cut the onion into quarters, then slice into thin wedges. Remove the long stems from the parsley, leaving the leafy clusters together.

Heat the oil in a small pan. Once hot, keep over medium heat. Drop the carrot clusters, onion wedges, and parsley sprigs into the batter one at a time. With a tablespoon, slide them into the deep hot oil. Take them out with a fork when golden brown and drain them on absorbent paper. Serve with a small dish of soy sauce. Serves three.

Note: Chopsticks can be inexpensively purchased at a restaurant supply store.

Games from Japan

Jan Ken Pon

In the United States, this game is called "Scissors, Paper, Stone." It is one of the first games that Japanese children learn. To play the game, two players face one another. They say together, "*Jan ken pon.*" (The words "jan ken pon" mean about the same as "eeny meeny miney mo.") When they say, "Pon," they make either the scissors, paper, or stone symbol with their hands, just as Americans do in their version of the game. (**Note:** In Japanese, the word for stone is *gu,* scissors is *choki,* and paper is *pa.*)

If there is a tie in Jan Ken Pon, then the players say, "*Ai kono sho.*" On "sho," they make one of the three hand symbols again.

Crab Relay

Form two teams. One at a time, each player on a team must move to a predetermined goal and back by walking like a crab. To do so, the players sit on the floor and use their hands and feet to lift and move their bodies. The first team to finish the relay wins.

Japanese Baseball

The number one sport in Japan is baseball. It is played exactly like American baseball, except the field is slightly smaller.

Professional Japanese baseball teams are owned by large companies. For example the Seibu Lions are owned by the Seibu Department Stores, and the Yo Mi Uri Giants are owned by the Yo Mi Uri newspaper.

To play Japanese baseball, divide the class into two baseball teams. Name one the Seibu Lions and the other the Yo Mi Uri Giants. Then, play ball!

Name_____

Haiku

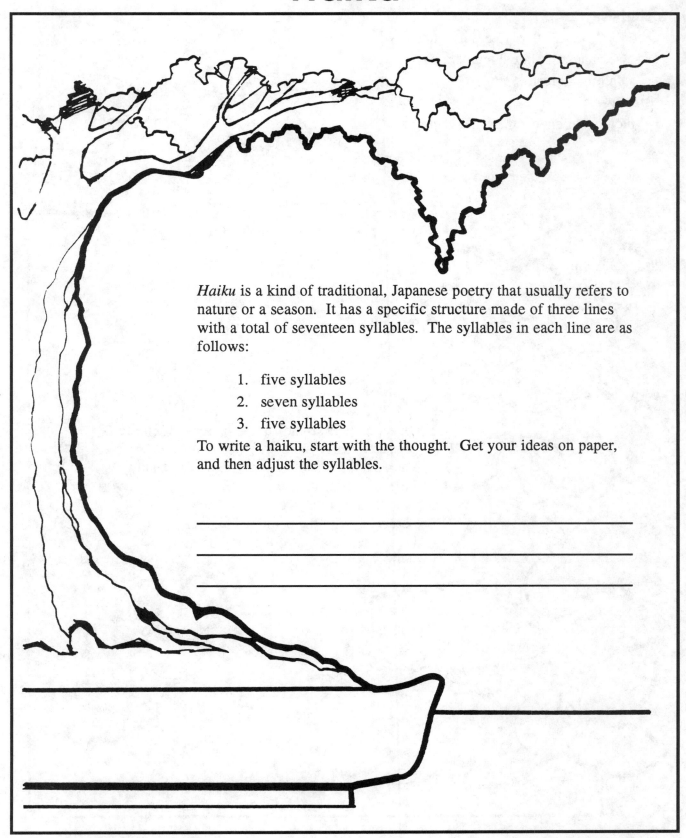

Haiku is a kind of traditional, Japanese poetry that usually refers to nature or a season. It has a specific structure made of three lines with a total of seventeen syllables. The syllables in each line are as follows:

1. five syllables
2. seven syllables
3. five syllables

To write a haiku, start with the thought. Get your ideas on paper, and then adjust the syllables.

_____

_____

_____

Cherry Blossom Art

Materials:

- 5" x 7" (12.5 cm x 17.5 cm) white paper
- black and pink liquid tempera paint
- small paintbrush
- straw
- pictures of cherry trees and cherry blossoms

Directions: First, look at the pictures of cherry trees and cherry blossoms. Then, put a drop of black paint at the bottom of the paper. Using the straw, blow the paint gently in various directions to create the look of a branch. With the paintbrush, gently dab a small amount of the pink paint on the black branch.

Community Ties

1. **Flag Patterns:** Pages 32 and 33 provide patterns for both the Japanese flag and the U.S. flag. Use them to create a bulletin board for this unit of study. At the top of the board, write "Sharing Our World." Color and display the two flags. Then have the students draw or cut from magazines pictures of things the two nations have in common. Use the bulletin board as a springboard for writing activities and other projects about the similarities among peoples around the world. (You can easily extend the bulletin board idea to include other nations as well.)

2. **Sights and Sounds of Our Town:** Pages 34 and 35 require the students to take a walking tour of the school neighborhood. These activities will allow the students to become familiar with the community while also using their senses of sight and hearing. Additionally, the graph will reinforce math skills.

   To complete the worksheets, have the students tour the immediate school neighborhood. Individuals, partners, or teams, can tally the various things they see and hear while on their tour. Use the charts as they are, or blank out the provided items and have the students fill those in as well.

   Use this information back in the classroom for discussion or for writing activities. You might also use the information gained to create a classroom mural entitled, "Sights and Sounds of Our Neighborhood." Students can make audiotape recordings of real neighborhood sounds or simulated ones and place the recordings next to the mural. If students simulate the sounds, be sure to make the connection between their simulations and Crow Boy's recreation of the "voices of crows."

3. **Meet Kristi Yamaguchi:** Page 36 offers interesting information about this Japanese-American figure skater. Students will be able to see how Ms. Yamaguchi overcame many obstacles to fulfill her dreams. Her story will prove inspirational to them.

4. **Kristi Crossword:** This crossword on page 37 uses the information learned from page 36.

5. **Map Kristi's Day:** After completing this map activity on page 38, the students can make maps of their own days. Share them with a partner or in small groups. In this way, students can find out more about the similarities and differences among themselves and their peers.

6. **Whose Shoe?:** This fun and simple activity on page 39 will also allow students to make connections among people—both what they have in common and the differences within their commonalities.

   The activity may be expanded by taking pictures of the students' feet and then making a learning center. On index cards, write each child's name and see if the students can match the shoe to the person.

   You might also, just for fun, play the game in which all the students (or groups of students) put their shoes in a pile in the middle of the floor, stand against the walls of the classroom, and then at "Go!" run to the pile to find their shoes.

Flag Patterns

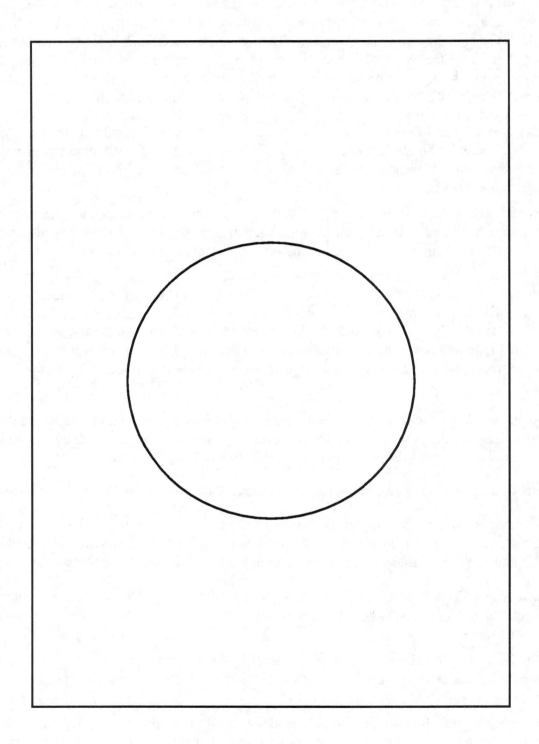

Japan

Source of the Sun

Flag Patterns *(cont.)*

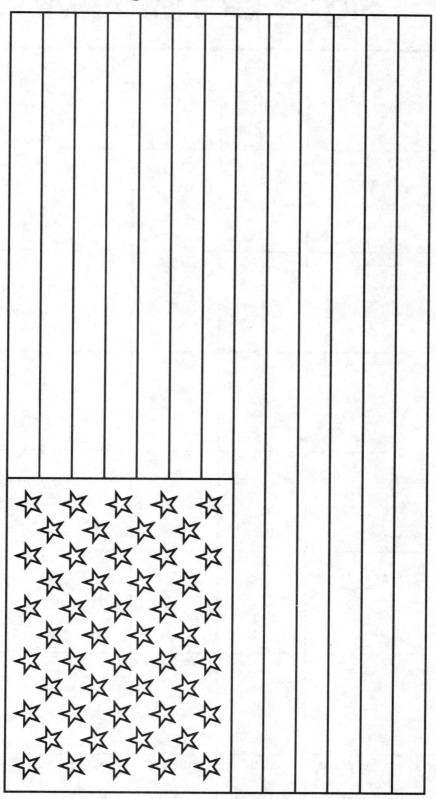

The United States
Home of the Free and the Brave

Name_____

Sights of Our Town

	Trees	Flowers	Birds	Insects	Cats	Dogs	Other
7 or more							
6							
5							
4							
3							
2							
1							

Name_____

Sounds of Our Town

	People	Cars	Airplanes	Trucks	Birds	Mammals	Other
7 or more							
6							
5							
4							
3							
2							
1							

Name_____

Profile on Kristi Yamaguchi

Directions: Read the following information about Kristi Yamaguchi. Then fill in the blanks in the statements that follow.

Meet Kristi Yamaguchi

Born in Fremont, California, Kristi Yamaguchi is a world champion figure skater and the first Japanese American to become a sports superstar. She began figure skating at the age of six and has consistently demonstrated the persistence that has made her a champion.

Kristi has had to overcome difficulties all her life. She was born with a condition known as "clubfeet" and had to undergo surgery that would align her feet correctly with her legs. It is amazing that an athlete with such grace of movement began her life with a handicapping condition.

When Kristi was in high school, she (like Crow Boy) had to wake up very early in the morning to begin her day. Just after 4:00 A.M., she would begin skating for five hours, perfecting her jumps and spins. She would then attend afternoon classes at Mission San Jose High School. While most teenagers were going on dates and working part-time, Kristi spent her free time alone on the ice. One day, her classmates would realize that the sacrifices she made were worth their weight in gold.

All of Kristi's hard work paid off. In 1991, she won the World Figure Skating Championship. Then in 1992, at the Olympics in Albertville, France, she won the gold medal for figure skating.

It is interesting to remember that Kristi Yamaguchi, the figure skating champion, is also Kristi Yamaguchi, young American woman. In many ways, her life is just like that of many others. She is a fourth generation American. (Her parents and her grandparents were born in the United States.) She has a younger brother and an older sister. Her father is a dentist. Her family belongs to a Buddhist temple. In these ways, her life is typical. What is not so typical is her championship status. However, even with that, she is in one way just like everyone else. Everyone has the ability within to shine. What has made Kristi special is her determination to succeed.

1. Kristi began skating at the age of _____.

2. Kristi won a _____ medal in the Olympics.

3. Kristi is the first _____ American to become a sports superstar.

Kristi Crossword

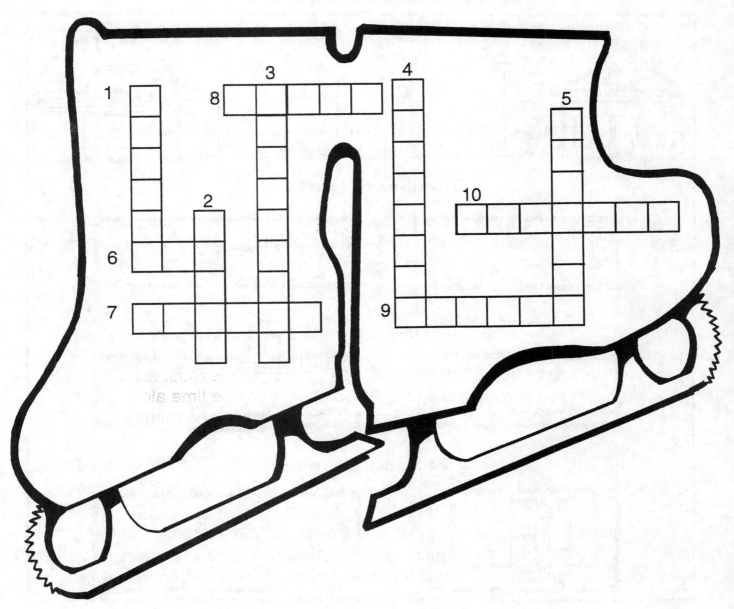

Across

6. Kristi skates on _____.
7. A good _____ must practice everyday.
8. Kristi's favorite _____ is ice skating.
9. She has an older _____.
10. Her father is a _____.

Down

1. _____ Yamaguchi is a skating champion.
2. Kristi won a gold _____.
3. Kristi _____ skating before school.
4. In 1992, Kristi was in the _____.
5. Kristi's _____ is younger than she.

Name_____

Map Kristi's Day

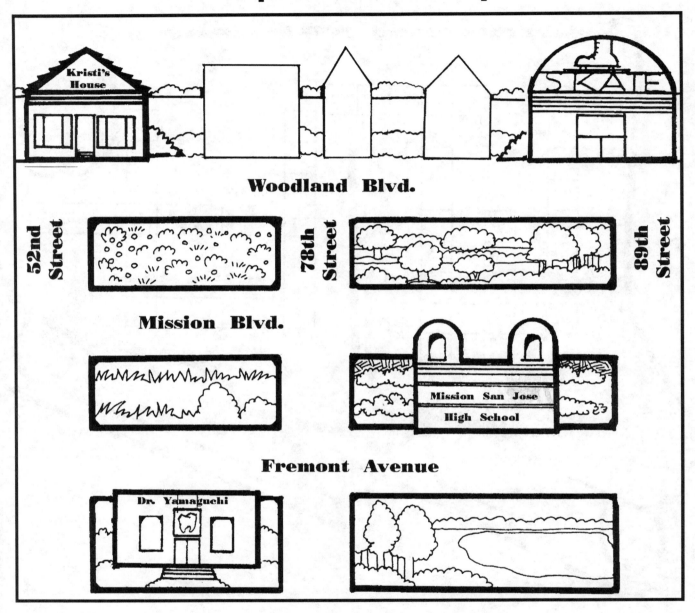

Directions: Draw lines on the map according to the directions below.

1. Draw a line east from Kristi's home to the skating arena.

2. Draw a line one block south and then one-half block west to Kristi's high school.

3. Draw a line west on Mission Boulevard and then south on 78th Street to Dr. Yamaguchi's office.

4. Draw a line west on Fremont Avenue and north on 52nd Street to Kristi's house.

Name_____

Whose Shoe?

Directions: Match the shoe to the person who wears it. Then, draw the shoe you are wearing today.

zori	**tennis shoe**	**ice skate**
Kristi Yamaguchi	**American child**	**Crow Boy**

my shoe

The Legend of the Indian Paintbrush: Summing It Up

Little Gopher is the smallest Indian boy in his tribe. He is unable to keep up with the other boys who run, shoot bows, and prove their strength. However, he does have a special ability as an artist. The *shaman* of the tribe tells him that though he will not grow up to be a great warrior, he will be remembered honorably by his people for a different reason.

A Dream-Vision tells Little Gopher that he will become great among his people by painting pictures. He is told to find a white buckskin and to paint a picture of the evening sky on it. Instead of playing with the other boys and hunting, Little Gopher follows the message of his Dream-Vision. He begins to paint pictures for his people, searching for the right plants to provide the vibrant colors of the sunset. He keeps a white buckskin at the ready for the time when the colors are made available.

One night, a voice tells him that because he has been faithful to his people, he will find the colors. The next evening he finds them on paintbrushes growing from a hillside. He paints the sunset, leaving the brushes where he has found them. In the morning, the hill where the brushes grew is covered with the wildflower now known as Indian paintbrush.

Getting to Know the Author and Illustrator

Tomie dePaola is an internationally known artist and author of children's books. He was born in Meriden, Connecticut, and now lives in New Hampshire. He received a B.F.A. at Pratt Institute in Brooklyn and an M.F.A. at California College of Arts and Crafts. Mr. dePaola taught art and theater for a number of years, but now devotes his time to writing and illustrating children's books.

Mr. dePaola is perhaps most noted for his warmth, good humor, and positive spirit. His love of people and life seems to fill the pages of his books. For these reasons, together with his enormous talent, Tomie dePaola is one of today's most popular and well-loved author/artists.

Mr. dePaola has illustrated over one-hundred and sixty books. He loves art so much that he considers himself to be an artist first and then an author. The illustrations that appear in *The Legend of the Indian Paintbrush* are typical of his style. He likes to draw images that are simple and direct, describing his style as a mixture of Romanesque and folk. Like the main character of the story, Mr. dePaola spends a lot of time searching for just the right colors. One day, he, too, would like to stumble upon a hill filled with brushes of the exact colors he needs.

Getting Started

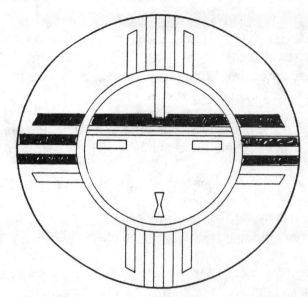

1. **What We Know:** Prepare a large chart with two columns. The title of the chart will be *Native Americans*. One column will be headed "What We Know," and the other column will be "What We Want to Know." The class will then brainstorm thoughts, facts, and questions that they may have regarding the subject.

   This chart will provide the teacher with an understanding of the students' prior knowledge. It will also serve as a guide for what the students want to learn. This chart is to be saved and periodically reviewed throughout the unit.

   Note: Please keep in mind that the group of people called Native Americans is made of unique individuals and diverse cultures. Be wary of blanket statements and stereotypes, and be sensitive to the fact that "Native American" is a label given to real, living people who are as varied as the groups called "Asian American," "African American," "Hispanics," and so on.

2. **History of the Plains Indians:** Share the following information with the class. (If possible, bring in Native American speakers to discuss the lives of Indians today.)

   The Great Plains of North America reach from central Texas northward into Canada and from the Rocky Mountains eastward to the Mississippi River. For thousands of years, buffalo (or bison) roamed the open grasslands freely, and small bands of roving hunters depended on the herds. These were the Plains Indians.

   In the north, there lived such tribes as the Assiniboin, Blackfoot, Crow, Gros Ventre, Plains-Crow, Plains-Ojibway, Sarsi, and Teton-Dakota. In the south, the tribes included the Arapaho, Comanche, Cheyenne, Kiowa, and Kiowa-Apache. The east housed the Arikara, Hidatsa, Iowa, Kansa, Mandan, Missouri, Omaha, Osage, Oto, Pawnee, Ponca, Eastern Dakota, and Wichita, among others. And in the west dwelled such tribes as the Bannock, Nez Perce, Northern Shoshoni, Ute, and Wind River Shoshoni.

   Many of the these tribes are intrinsic to the history of the western United States. Their cultures were often centered around the buffalo or bison. These great animals provided the tribes with all of their basic necessities, including food, shelter, and clothing. The tribes used bows and arrows to kill the bison even after guns had been introduced to their region. Bows could be made from the horns of a mountain sheep, and the arrowheads were made from stone. The meat could be preserved by cutting it into strips, placing it in boiling water for a few moments, and then drying it in the sun.

Getting Started *(cont.)*

Prior to the 16th century, the nomadic tribes traveled on foot. Sleds were used to carry large equipment, and dogs pulled them. By the mid 1600's, the Apaches had acquired horses from the Spanish explorer Francisco Vasquez de Coronado. By the late 1700's, the horse culture had been spread throughout the central plains.

Life for the tribes was transformed by the combination of horses, firearms, and trade with Europeans. The tribes became more nomadic in their search for buffalo, and this led to conflicts over land.

By this time, the numbers of European immigrants were growing, bringing with them their different beliefs and values. Fundamental to many Native Americans was the belief that the land could not be owned, but rather offered its bounty to people for their nourishment. Many Europeans, however, believed that the land was theirs for the taking, to own and tame for their livelihoods.

From 1780 until 1838, a smallpox epidemic (acquired from the influx of Europeans) swept across the plains. Thousands of Native Americans perished from this deadly disease. Meanwhile, the American government and its citizens thirsted for the ownership of more land, and bit by bit the Indians were moved aside and even killed. In 1825, the Kansa and Osage ceded almost 100 million acres of land to the United States. Then in 1830, President Andrew Jackson signed the Indian Removal Act which authorized the removal of the eastern tribes to Indian Territory (land west of Missouri and Arkansas). From 1830 until 1850, numerous treaties were signed and then broken by the United States government. The treaties were legal weapons used by the government to appropriate Indian lands and confine tribes to shrinking areas. In 1851, the Indian Appropriation Act legalized reservations, and more than 50 tribes were sent to Indian Territory between 1859 and 1860. In 1905, five tribes pressed for their own state, Sequoyah, but Congress soon voted Indian Territory a part of Oklahoma State. By this time, all surviving tribes were permanently located on reservations.

These strikes to the ways of life for many Native Americans have often proved devastating and debilitating. However, the spirit of the people has lived on. Our current times see a push for understanding and value of Native American perspectives and culture. The tribes themselves seem to be celebrating their own cultures with a renewed vigor, and many tribes are growing stronger than ever before. Modern leaders, such as Wilma Mankiller, and educators, such as Virginia Driving Hawk Sneve, are helping to bring about a strength and health that, with hope and energy, may heal the old wounds.

People Are People

The purpose of these lessons is to teach the children the importance of sticking to a task and trying to be the best that they can be. Little Gopher wanted to play with the other boys, but he was talented enough to be a great artist and felt guided to pursue that calling. The activities in this section will help the children decide what their strengths and weaknesses are and help provide them with the motivation to complete a task.

1. **Feelings:** After hearing the story, ask the children how they think Little Gopher felt when he watched the other boys play. Their responses should include "lonely" and "left out." Then ask them if they have ever felt that way themselves, either at home or at school. Allow them time to share their feelings.

2. **Following a Dream-Vision:** When Little Gopher receives his Dream-Vision, it is not easy for him to forego some of the desires of his heart in order to pursue it. Yet he does. Ask the children to offer some reasons why he does. Also, discuss the good that comes to Little Gopher because he follows his guidance. (He is able to paint the sunset, the flowers grow, and he is remembered by his people.)

   Explain to the children that the Plains Indians of the time were religious people who believed in Dream-Visions. A Dream-Vision was thought to be a message from the gods. The Plains Indians made decisions about their lives according to what was revealed in a vision. Sometimes a Dream-Vision would tell a person to do things that he/she did not want to do, but because of his/her beliefs, that person would carry out the deeds.

   Let the children know that sometimes they will have to do something that they may not want to do, but in the end something good may come out of their hard work. Give them examples of things they must do at school that they may not always want to do (such as read or do math), but in the end they will benefit from having completed the task. Tell them that they can learn from Little Gopher. It may be difficult at times to complete a task, but in the end something good will happen for them.

3. **My Dream-Vision:** Ask the students to write and/or draw predictions for their own Dream-Visions. Share them as a class or in small groups.

4. **I Can't/I Can:** Page 44 can be used to check comprehension of the story and to help the students identify what they can do well.

5. **Meet Little _____ :** Page 45 will help the students discover their likes and dislikes. You can later use the information from this page for a writing activity.

6. **Fold Book:** Have the students use the seven circled or completed statements from page 45, as well as a title, to fill the eight-page book they can create by following the directions on page 46. Illustrate and color as desired.

7. **Words That Won't Quit:** To foster self-motivation, provide the students with page 47. This page lists motivational phrases and encourages the children to incorporate the phrases with tasks they must do but do not like to do. The phrases can be posted in the room or taped to each student's desk.

Name_____

I Can't/I Can

Directions: Fill in the blanks with the words below.

gift   run   warriors   paint

1. Little Gopher cannot _____ like the other boys.
2. Little Gopher can _____.
3. The other boys will one day be _____.
4. Little Gopher has a _____ that is special.

Directions: Fill in the blanks with words that make sense for you.

1. At home, I cannot _____.
   But I can _____.
2. At school, I cannot _____.
   But I can _____.
3. During recess, I cannot _____.
   But I can _____.
4. My special gift is _____.

Name_____

Meet Little _____
(your name)

Directions: Circle the sentence that best describes you in numbers one through four. Fill in the blanks for number five.

1. I enjoy talking to people.

   I enjoy listening to people.

   I enjoy both listening and talking to people.

2. I prefer to watch teams play.

   I prefer to play on a team.

   I do not like team activities.

3. I like to be indoors.

   I like to be outdoors.

   I like being indoors and being outdoors.

4. I like to sing.

   I like to dance.

   I like to make my own music.

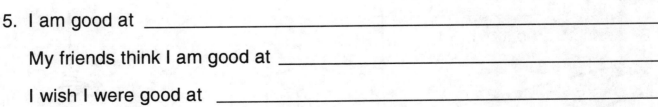

5. I am good at _____.

   My friends think I am good at _____.

   I wish I were good at _____.

Fold Book

Directions:

1. Fold a sheet of paper in half lengthwise.

2. Fold in half again.

3. Fold in half again.

4. Unfold the paper. You will now have eight parts.

5. Fold in half widthwise.

6. Cut or tear along the center crease from the folded edge to the next fold.

7. Open the paper.

8. Fold it lengthwise again.

9. Push the end sections together to fold into a little book.

10. There will be eight pages in all.

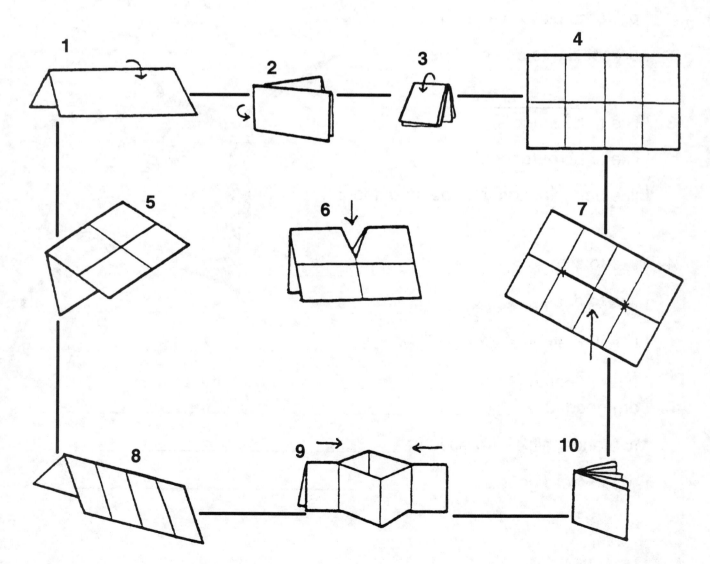

Name_____

Words That Won't Quit

Directions: Match the words to make motivational phrases. Rewrite each new phrase.

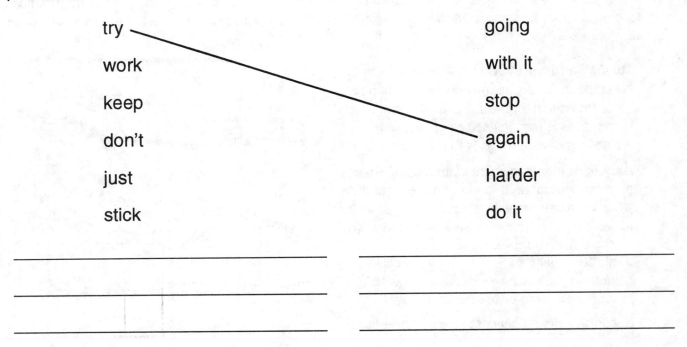

try	going
work	with it
keep	stop
don't	again
just	harder
stick	do it

_____   _____

_____   _____

_____   _____

Directions: Complete the sentences with words that make sense for you. On the first line, make up your own word. On the second line, use a phrase from above.

1. At school, sometimes I don't want to_____.

   I have to remember to _____.

2. At home, sometimes I don't want to _____.

   I have to remember to _____.

Socializing Skills Project: Keeping a Promise

In the story, Little Gopher agrees to paint instead of trying to play with the other boys in his tribe. In a sense, he has made a promise. In this mini-unit, your students will learn three things: the importance of keeping a promise, how to decide whether or not to make a promise, and the fact that sometimes people break promises.

1. **How Would You Feel?:** Discuss with the class the meaning of "promise." Explain to them that when a promise is made, the person who makes it is supposed to do or give whatever he/she promises to do or give.

   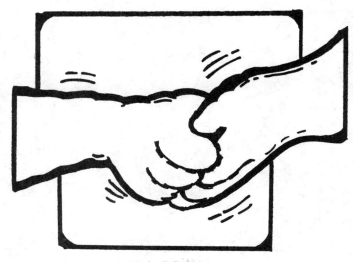

   Ask the students to share examples of when a promise was made to them and kept and then when a promise was made to them and broken. Make a two-column chart on the board. Write on the left, "Promises Kept," and write on the right, "Promises Broken." Under each column, brainstorm the feelings felt when promises are kept or broken.

   Encourage the students to refer to this chart when they complete page 49.

2. **A Guide to Making Promises:** Before passing out page 50, share the following rule with your students. *Never make a promise that you are not willing to keep.* Have the students write this rule on page 50. Discuss the fact that a person must be true to his/her word in order for others to trust that person. Also discuss the fact that no one has to make a promise. It is all right to tell another person that you cannot do what that person wants you to do, or that you will try but you cannot make promises about the outcome.

   Now, discuss with the students that a promise means doing what you said you would do and giving what you said you would give. Have the students fill in this information on page 50. Once again, do not make any promise that you are not sure you want to make. Making a promise is a personal choice.

   In the third section of page 50, the students will write these two questions: (1) Do I want to make this promise? and (2) Can I really keep this promise? Never make a promise without first answering yes to both these questions.

   The fourth section of page 50 considers the consequences of breaking a promise. Students should know that if they break a promise, they will probably not be trusted. They will disappoint others, and others will feel that they cannot count on them. Have the students fill in the blanks of the fourth section with this information.

3. **A Promise You Can Keep:** On this page, students can consider realistic and unrealistic promises. Discuss after completion or do as a class.

Name_____

How Would You Feel?

Directions: Write how you would feel on the line after each sentence.

1. Your friend promises to let you play with the soccer ball, but you wait all recess and never get a turn.

   _____

2. Your grandmother promises to take you to the movies. She takes you, and you get to choose the movie.

   _____

3. Your brother promises to fix your bike, but when you need it the tire is still flat.

   _____

4. Your teacher promises to let you sharpen the pencils for the class, but you see her letting somebody else sharpen the pencils.

   _____

5. You promise to let your friend spend the night, but your mother says, "No."

   _____

6. Your friend promises to share his/her snack, and at recess he/she does.

   _____

7. Your sister promises to save you a piece of her candy, but when you get home, she has eaten it all.

   _____

8. You promise to finish your homework, but you fall asleep while watching television.

   _____

Name_____

A Guide to Making Promises

Rule:

_____

_____

_____

_____

_____

_____

1. A promise is _____

    _____

    _____

    _____

    _____.

2. A promise is _____

    _____

    _____

    _____

    _____

    _____.

Before making a promise, ask yourself the following questions.

1. _____

    _____

    _____

    _____

2. _____

    _____

    _____

    _____

Your answer to both should be **YES!**

Remember:

1. If you break your promise, people will not _____ you.

2. You will _____ others.

3. Others will feel they cannot _____ on you.

Name_____

A Promise You Can Keep

Directions: Put a check next to the promises that the average person could realistically keep.

☐ I promise I'll share my book.

☐ I promise I'll give you a million dollars.

☐ I promise I'll bake you some cookies.

☐ I promise I'll let you swing after me.

☐ I promise I'll give you my brother's football jersey.

☐ I promise I'll let you have all my toys.

☐ I promise I'll help you with your homework.

☐ I promise I'll do your housework for a month.

☐ I promise I'll eat my lunch.

☐ I promise I'll do my best.

Directions: Use the code at the bottom of the page to figure out the secret message.

__ __ __ __ __   __ __ __ __   __   __ __ __ __ __ __ __
14 5 22 5 18 13 1 11 5   1   16 18 15 13 9 19 5

__ __ __   __ __ __   __ __ __   __ __ __ __ __ __ __
25 15 21   1 18 5   14 15 20   23 9 12 12 9 14 7

__ __   __ __ __ __
20 15   11 5 5 16

Code:

a	b	c	d	e	f	g	h	i	j	k	l	m
1	2	3	4	5	6	7	8	9	10	11	12	13

n	o	p	q	r	s	t	u	v	w	x	y	z
14	15	16	17	18	19	20	21	22	23	24	25	26

Getting from Here to There

The purpose of these lessons is to familiarize the students with maps and graphs, to teach them how to identify places on a map, and to show them how to read a bar graph.

1. **Buffalo Hunt:** Before completing page 53, it will be useful to provide the children with some information on the movement of the Plains Indians. Also, hold a quick review of cardinal directions. The children will need their knowledge of directions in order to fill in the missing words on page 53.

   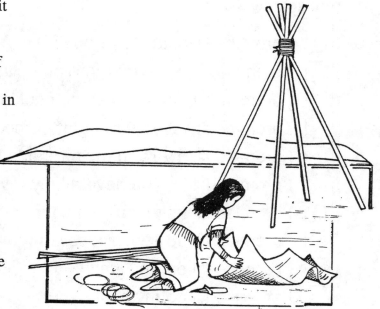

   Share with the students the following information:

   Because the Plains Indians depended on the buffalo for survival, they had to follow the herds. At first, they used dogs to help them carry their supplies. Later, the horse was introduced. Once they had horses, they were able to travel greater distances, averaging between ten and fifteen miles a day.

   The members of the tribes were always ready to move the camp quickly. If the chief gave the word to move, they could be packed and ready to go within a few minutes.

   One thing that made this quick move possible was the use of the tepee. *Tepee* comes from the Sioux language and means "dwelling." A tepee was made from buffalo skins and is considered to be one of the best designed tents in the history of humankind. It was capable of keeping out wind, rain, and snow, yet it was easy to transport and construct.

   The most common design for the tepee consisted of three poles which supported the buffalo hides. The poles were usually twenty to twenty-five foot (seven to nine meter) pine or cedar logs. Several skins were tanned and then sewn together to form a half circle. The women (who made, erected, and transported the tepees) would make a smoke flap and a circular opening for the door. When erecting a tepee, the three support poles were placed upright. These poles were secured, and several other poles were then stacked around the support poles. All of the poles were then tied together. The cover was tied to the back and then lifted onto the frame. It was then unrolled around the frame. At the doorway, a separate hide was used for the door.

2. **A Moving Village:** Depending on the ability of the students, the graph on page 54 can be completed independently or with your guidance. For a challenge, link pages 53 and 54 by tracing the information from the graph onto the map.

Name_____

Buffalo Hunt

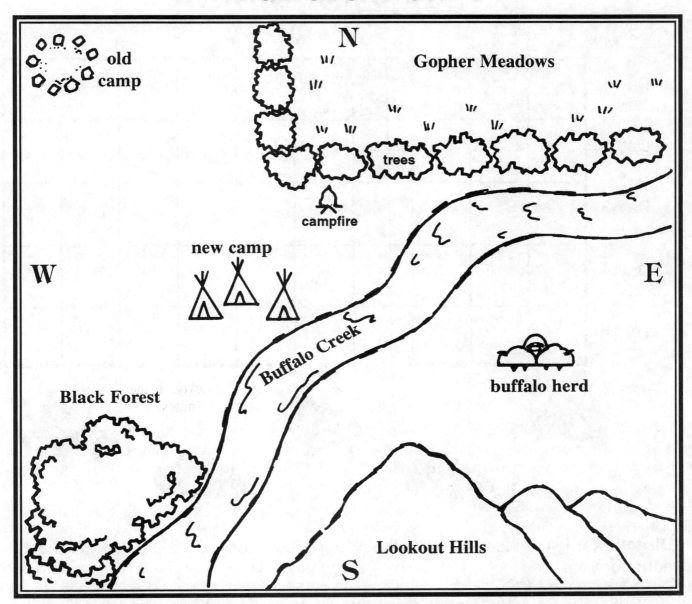

Directions: Use the information from the map to fill in the blanks below.

1. East of Buffalo Creek is _____ and _____.

2. To get from the old camp to Gopher Meadow, go_____.

3. Lookout Hills are _____ of Gopher Meadow.

4. The buffalo herd is _____of Lookout Hills.

5. The Black Forest and the new camp are _____of Buffalo Creek.

Name_____

A Moving Village

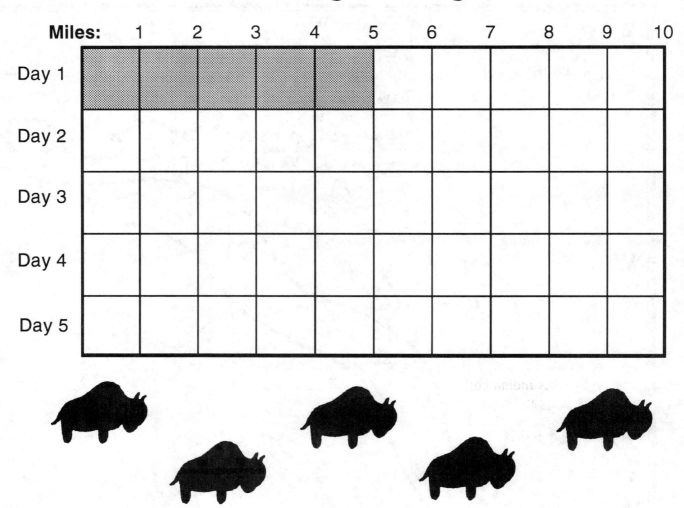

Directions: Fill in the graph with the information below. The first one has been done for you.

1. Buffalo are spotted east of the camp in Gopher Meadow. The village packs up and moves five miles before the sun sets.

2. The village gets an early start and follows the herd south for ten miles.

3. The village moves seven miles to Buffalo Creek when a rainstorm forces them to stop.

4. It rains all day so the village does not move.

5. The village walks two miles to the shallow part of Buffalo Creek. After crossing the creek, the people walk four more miles to Lookout Hills.

Experiencing the Culture

The next exercises are designed to teach the students about the lives of Plains Indians in the past and the present.

1. **Living in a Tepee:** Before doing this true-or-false worksheet on page 58, review the information on page 52 about tepees. (See "Buffalo Hunt.")

2. **Reservation Life:** Use page 59 to teach the children about reservations. You may want to arrange a field trip to a reservation if one is located close to you. If you are located on a reservation, take this opportunity to investigate its history.

3. **Build a House:** Page 60 is designed to help the students link the last two pages together.

4. **Shared Values:** It is common in Native American tradition to value the earth. Native Americans believe that one does not own the land. The earth is seen as mother and the sky as father. They also believe that there is an intimate link between earth and man.

   Page 61 will give the children a chance to identify the parts of the world that come from the earth and sky. Then, they can evaluate the importance of the earth and the sky, connecting their values with traditional Native American values.

5. **Plains Indian Games:** The purpose of the games on page 62 is to familiarize the students with the play of Plains Indian children of the past. Though Indian boys and girls rarely played together, these games can be played by the entire class.

6. **Working Together:** Explain to the students that in order for a tribe to survive, everyone had a role to play. Today, every working community also has roles that individuals must fill so that all may live comfortably. Discuss with the class the roles in your community. Also, discuss the roles in your classroom.

   As a class, prepare to become an interdependent "tribe." Explain that everyone must work together to do the daily classroom tasks. As a class, list on a large sheet of chart paper all the tasks that must be done throughout the course of the day. You may have already assigned classroom monitors, so refer to those jobs for ideas.

   It is important for each student to have a job. In order to create a job for everyone, some jobs can be broken into smaller tasks. For example, the paper monitor job can be divided into a paper monitor for each subject, or the pencil sharpener job can be divided into a morning and afternoon position.

   Remind the children that although Little Gopher wanted to play with the other boys, he did not because he had a different job to do. Explain that everyone will not be able to do his/her first job choice. Assign the jobs either randomly, according to an already established roster, or by having students volunteer.

Experiencing the Culture *(cont.)*

Have everyone become responsible for his/her task on the following morning. In order to remember who does what, use the "Pop-Up Name Tag" (page 63). Tell the children that the Plains Indians were sometimes named according to something that they could do. When the students assume their tasks, have each write his/her new name on the name tag. (For example, the paper collector will be "Paper Collector," the window opener will be "Window Opener," and so forth.) During the next day, remember to address the children according to their new titles.

At the end of the day, ask the children how they thought things went with each person having a job to do. If the class enjoyed this, you may consider switching from a monitor system that only includes a few children each week to one that includes all the class. A permanent job chart can be made, and each week the name at the top of the list will go to the bottom, and each child will move up to the next job.

7. **Contribution Puzzle:** The class can make a puzzle which will show what each member contributes to the room. For example, Thuy is an artist, Carla helps others with math, and so forth. Each student will fill in a puzzle piece describing (or drawing) what he or she is good at. Put the pieces together around the walls of the room. Use page 64 as a pattern for the puzzle piece.

8. **Match the Dresses:** This activity will show the children a variety of dress styles made by various Plains Indian tribes. After completing page 65, the students can draw their own pictures of people wearing these styles. They can then try to guess which tribe the person is from according to the dress in the picture.

9. **Silent Talking**: All the Plains tribes were able to communicate with universal hand symbols (sign language). Teach the children some of those symbols by using page 66. Practice until everyone knows them well. You may even make up some of your own.

   After the students learn the hand signs, explain to them that the Plains Indians also communicated with pictures. Find the page in *The Legend of the Indian Paintbrush* where Little Gopher paints pictures of great hunts and deeds. Ask them to "read" what happened in each picture. Then, give each student a copy of page 66 so they can see the pictures that go with the signs they have learned.

   The students can also combine words with the pictographs to write a rebus story. Write a class rebus first to model.

10. **Indian Recipes:** The recipes found on page 67 are simple enough to do in the classroom. However, to involve the parents, you may wish to send home the beef jerky recipe, offering extra credit to those students who made the jerky at home.

    Perhaps some parents may have their own recipes that use venison or beef. Make copies of any variations of the jerky recipes that you find. Allow the children to make a small recipe book.

Experiencing the Culture (cont.)

11. **Artistic Expressions:** The students can look through old magazines to find pictures of sunsets, and then they can make a sunset collage. Or, they can paint their own sunset using watercolors or fingerpaints.

    Alternately, students can experiment with dyes and dyeing by following the tips and directions on page 68.

12. **Parfleche:** Every Plains Indian had a parfleche, a container made of rawhide. It resembled an envelope and was used for carrying food, tools, clothing, and anything that needed to be stored while not in use. To make a small parfleche, use the pattern on page 69. A parfleche can be made out of construction paper, laminated construction paper, or felt. Decorate it with patterns like those found in *The Legend of the Indian Paintbrush* or any other patterns that you might like.

13. **Buffalo Game:** The purpose of this game is to teach the children the variety of uses the Plains Indians had for the buffalo. Before setting up the game, read all the game cards to the class and discuss each item and its use. You may ask the children what items we use today that are similar to the items the Plains Indians used long ago. You will find the game on pages 70-73. Laminate the gameboard so that it will last longer.

14. **Bulletin Board Ideas:** The students can create a learning board that shows the many uses the Plains Indians had for buffalo. Refer to the game on pages 70-73 to get ideas. Enlarge and duplicate the gameboard. Allow the children to draw some of the items to be posted on the board.

15. **Fair Trade:** The Plains Indians were able to meet most of their basic needs by hunting and growing a few crops. However, when there was something else they needed, they would trade with other tribes for the items. For example, the porcupine quills used to decorate garments were hard to come by in the Plains regions, so the Indians would trade.

    When Europeans first came to America, they traded horses for items the Native Americans had. Then the tribes began to trade the horses they had obtained. Eventually, they traded with the Europeans for guns, glass beads, and clothing materials.

    The economy of the Indians was based on trade. To experience this firsthand, designate one day as Trading Day. On this day, the children can bring items from home (with their parents' approval) for trade. To prepare for the day, discuss with the children the appropriate types of inexpensive trinkets that they can bring to school. Also, practice how to trade. Make sure they keep in mind the value of the items being traded. For example, ask if it would be fair to trade a pencil for a desk, or a broken crayon for a brand new crayon. Use page 74 to prepare for the lesson.

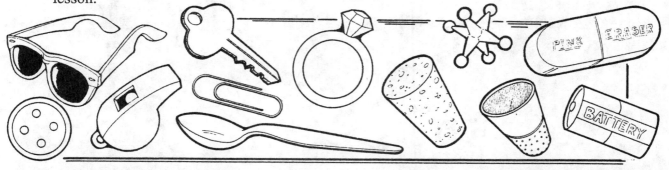

Name_____

Living in a Tepee

Little Gopher lives in a tepee. In fact, all of the Plains Indians used to live in tepees for at least part of the year. The tepee made a very comfortable home.

A tepee can keep out rain, snow, and cold air. It is made from buffalo hides. A dew cloth hangs from the side of the tepee to the ground, and it is decorated with symbols and pictures. Sometimes beads and quills are sewn to the cloth to make it very colorful.

The middle of the tepee is the cooking area. Along the walls there are leather boxes to hold clothes, toys, and tools. The floor is covered with animal furs.

Directions: After reading the information above, circle true or false for each statement below.

1. Snow goes right through a tepee.   **True**   **False**

2. A dew cloth is colorful.   **True**   **False**

3. Little Gopher lives in a tepee.   **True**   **False**

4. You cannot cook inside a tepee.   **True**   **False**

5. The floor of a tepee is covered with animal furs.   **True**   **False**

Name_____

Reservation Life

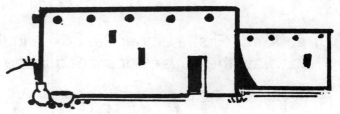

Many Native Americans live on reservations. A reservation is land the United States has set aside for the Native Americans. There are reservations in thirty-one states.

On a reservation you will see houses, stores, and roads. Some reservations have schools and museums. Most reservations have running water and electricity. Crafts and artwork are sometimes sold to visitors. The children on the reservations learn about their tribe's customs and beliefs. They also learn about life outside the reservation.

Directions: Read the information above, and then circle the correct answers below.

1. There are reservations in _____ states.
    A. 24
    B. 31
    C. 19

2. The _____ set aside land for the Native Americans.
    A. United States
    B. Indians
    C. visitors

3. Most reservations have electricity and _____.
    A. zoos
    B. beaches
    C. running water

4. Only some reservations have _____.
    A. tribes
    B. schools
    C. land

5. The Native Americans now usually live in _____.
    A. tepees
    B. stores
    C. houses

Name_____

Build a House

Directions: First, number the boxes in the order followed when making a tepee. Then, draw the houses described in the boxes below.

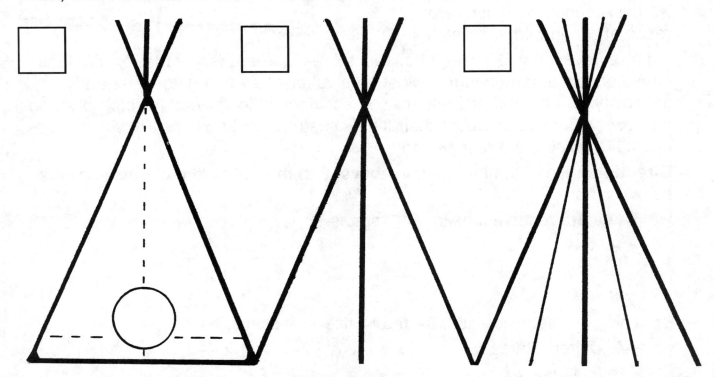

Draw your house.	Draw a house for a modern Native American.

Name_____

Shared Values

Many Native Americans value nature. It is important to them. They sometimes call the earth "Mother Earth" and the sky "Father Sky."

Directions: In box A, circle the items that come from Mother Earth. In box B, circle the items that come from Father Sky. Then, answer the questions.

Mother Earth   **Father Sky**

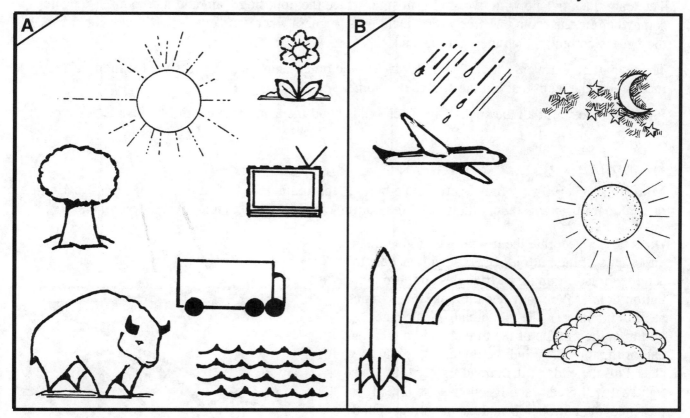

1. Why are the things on Mother Earth important? _____

_____

2. Why are the things in Father Sky important?_____

_____

3. What can we do to protect Mother Earth? _____

_____

4. How can we protect Father Sky? _____

_____

Plains Indian Games

Guessing Game

Materials: ten pencils or sticks

Directions: Divide the class into two groups. A person from each team comes forward and sits on the ground. A score stick (a pencil or stick) is given to each player, and each holds it in one hand behind his/her back. Flip a coin (or some such maneuver) to see who guesses first. Then, have that person try to guess which of his/her opponent's hands holds the stick. If he/she guesses correctly, he/she wins the stick. If not, then it is the other person's turn to guess.

The team that ends up with two sticks must now face the opposing team and hide both of the sticks somewhere in the room. The opposing team tries to guess where one of the two sticks is hidden. If they guess correctly, then they get the stick.

The team that just won a stick then hides it, and the other team tries to guess the location. If they guess incorrectly, the team that hid the stick gets another stick.

Play continues until all the sticks have been hidden and the team with the most sticks is declared the winner.

Humming Toy

Materials: 36" (90 cm) thread, a two-hole button (approximately 1.5" or 4 cm), two construction-paper or cardboard triangles (about the size of the button), sewing needle, and crayons or markers

Directions: Decorate the triangles and glue them to either side of the button. Use a sewing needle to run the thread through the triangles and through the button holes. (You may need to poke a few times to find the holes!) Tie the thread. Center the button in the middle of the thread and hold either end of the thread. Wind the thread as tightly as you can. Pull the ends of the thread tightly (but not so tightly it will break) and listen. As the thread unwinds, the button will make a humming sound.

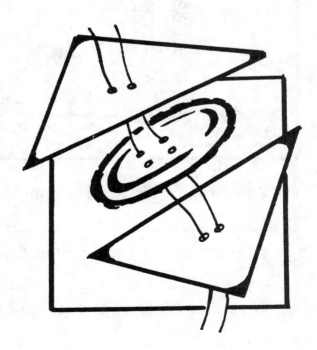

Repeat, but watch this time instead of listen. The decorated triangles will make interesting designs as they spin.

(Note: This is a great opportunity for a rudimentary discussion about energy, force, and motion.)

Pop-Up Name Tag

Directions: Cut on the solid line around the pattern. Cut around the sides and top of the Indian figure, leaving the bottom attached. Fold on the dotted line.

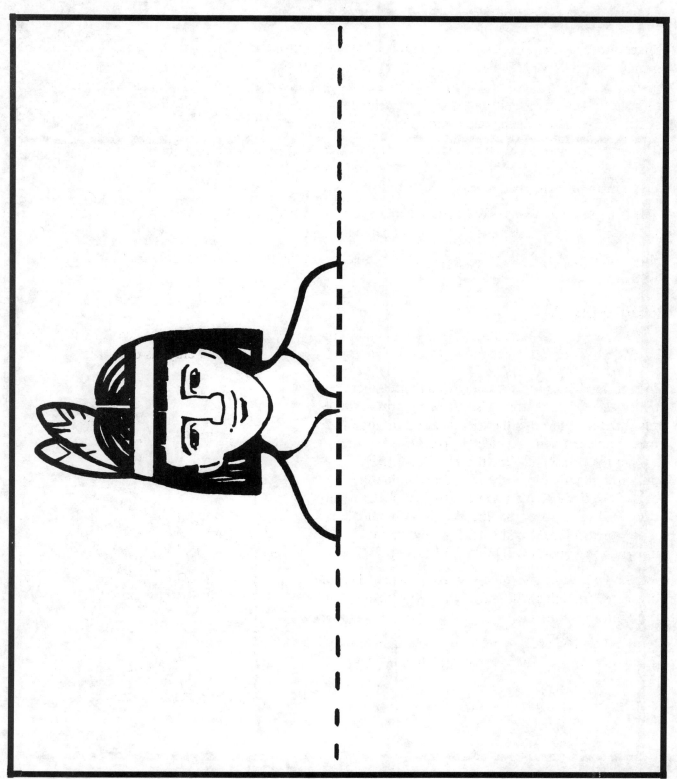

Contribution Puzzle

See page 56 for directions.

Name_____

Match the Dresses

Directions: Match the dresses. Color each pair the same.

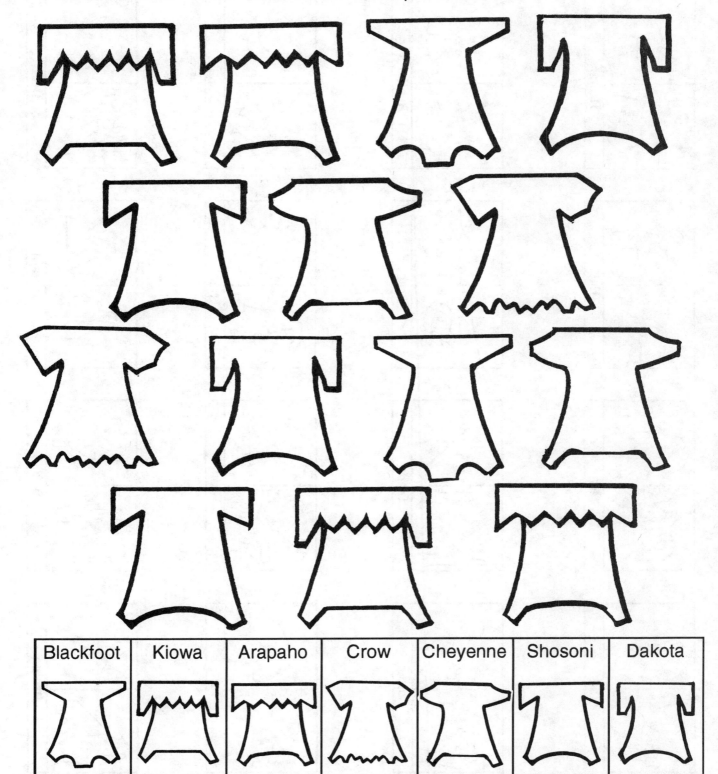

Blackfoot	Kiowa	Arapaho	Crow	Cheyenne	Shosoni	Dakota

Silent Talking

See page 56 for directions.

Indian Recipes

Children's Tea

Ingredients:

- 2 cups (500 mL) undiluted evaporated milk
- 2 cups (500 mL) hot water
- 2 teaspoons (10 mL) wild honey
- dash of cinnamon

Directions:

Mix all of the ingredients in a pitcher. Makes 4 servings.

Beef Jerky

Ingredients:

- 2 lbs. (1000 g) semi-frozen round, flank, or lean chuck steak
- 1 ½ tsps. (7.5 mL) *Liquid Smoke* (gives a wood-fire taste)
- 1 cup (250 mL) water
- 1 tsp. (5 mL) coarse salt
- 1 tsp. (5 mL) onion powder
- ½ tsp. (2.5 mL) garlic powder
- ½ tsp. (2.5 mL) ground black pepper
- ¼ cup (65 mL) soy sauce (optional)
- dash of Tabasco sauce (optional)

Directions:

Trim the fat from the meat. Mix all ingredients except the meat in a bowl. Slice the meat lengthwise along the grain in thin, long strips. Put the strips into the mixture and let them sit for two hours. Then, hang the strips from the rack in the oven. Set the oven at 200° F (95° C) or the lowest setting. Leave the oven door slightly open. When the strips become hard, dry, and black, they are ready. It will take about 24 hours.

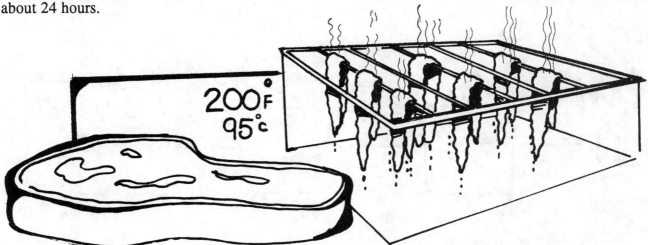

Artistic Expressions

Just as Little Gopher does, the students can experiment with various fruits and vegetables to find out what color dyes can be made from each item. Allow the children to predict what color each will produce.

The following items will make a natural dye when boiled in water:

- spinach leaves (green)
- onions (red or yellow)
- blackberries (blue)
- cranberries (red)
- carrots (orange)

Use any or all of these foods (and others) to make natural dyes.

Materials:

- variety of foods (See above.)
- water
- pot with a lid
- electric burner
- containers to hold the dyes

Optional Materials:

- food coloring
- white feathers
- macaroni
- 100% cotton fabric
- eggs

Directions: Mix three parts water to two parts food. Bring the mixture to a boil and let simmer for one and one-half hours. Remove from the heat. After the dye has cooled, remove the food and store the dye.

To dye an object such as a feather, fabric, or macaroni, place the object in the container with the dye. Add food coloring to make the dye brighter and longer lasting. To dye an egg, add a few teaspoons of vinegar.

Glue dyed feathers to two-inch (5 cm) wide construction paper strips and make a headdress. Use the dyed macaroni to make necklaces.

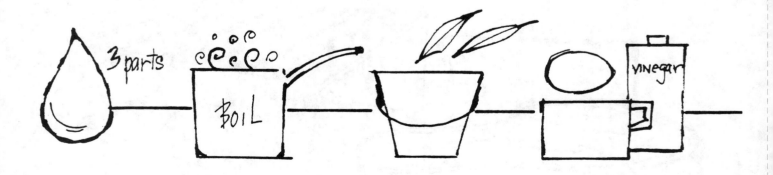

Parfleche

Directions: Cut on the solid lines (including the slit). Fold the sides of the parfleche back on the dotted lines. Fold the bottom up on the dotted line and glue over the sides. Fold the top down on the dotted line and insert the rounded edge into the slit. Decorate as desired.

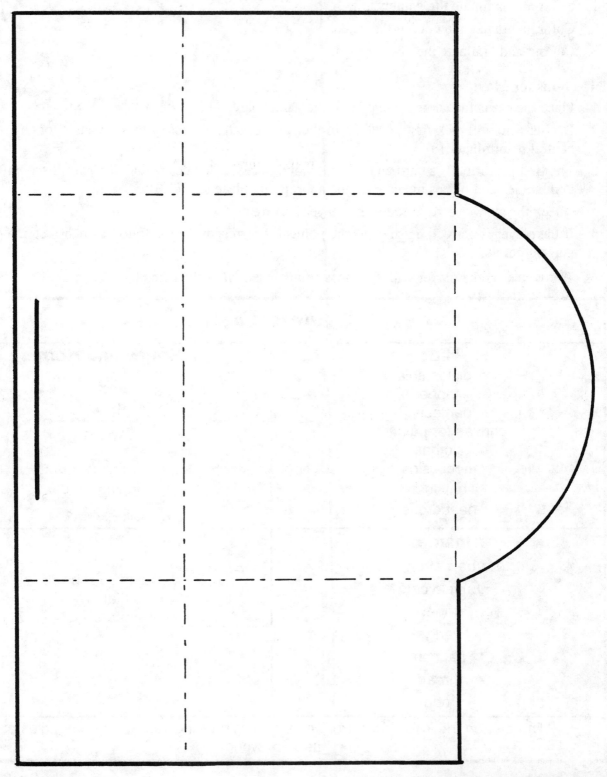

Buffalo Game

Materials: gameboard (page 71), 24 playing cards (pages 72-73), answer card (page 70), and a tally pad and pencil

Directions for Preparing the Game:

1. Color and laminate the gameboard.
2. Color, laminate, and cut out the cards.
3. Cut out and laminate the answer card.

Directions for Play:

1. Place the cards face down in a pile on the gameboard.
2. Decide who will pick first. (Play in birthday order, alphabetically by first name, or any other neutral determinant.)
3. The first player pulls a card and reads it aloud. He/she decides from what part of the buffalo the item comes and places the card on the appropriate place on the board.
4. Check the answer card to see if the player is correct.
5. If the player is correct, he/she gets the points on corresponding buffalo. If incorrect, the player gets no points.
6. The winner is the player with the most points when all of the cards have been drawn.

Answer Card	
Hide medicine shield tepee parfleche canvas for painting clothes moccasins bullboat headdress	**Bones and Horns** dice bowl knife* spoon digging hoe* sling shot*
Insides bow string buffalo chip meat jerky paunch thread rope	**Hair** bridle buffalo robe buffalo rug headdress
The hair on the knife is not from a buffalo. The slingshot and hoe handles are made of wood.	

Buffalo Game *(cont.)*

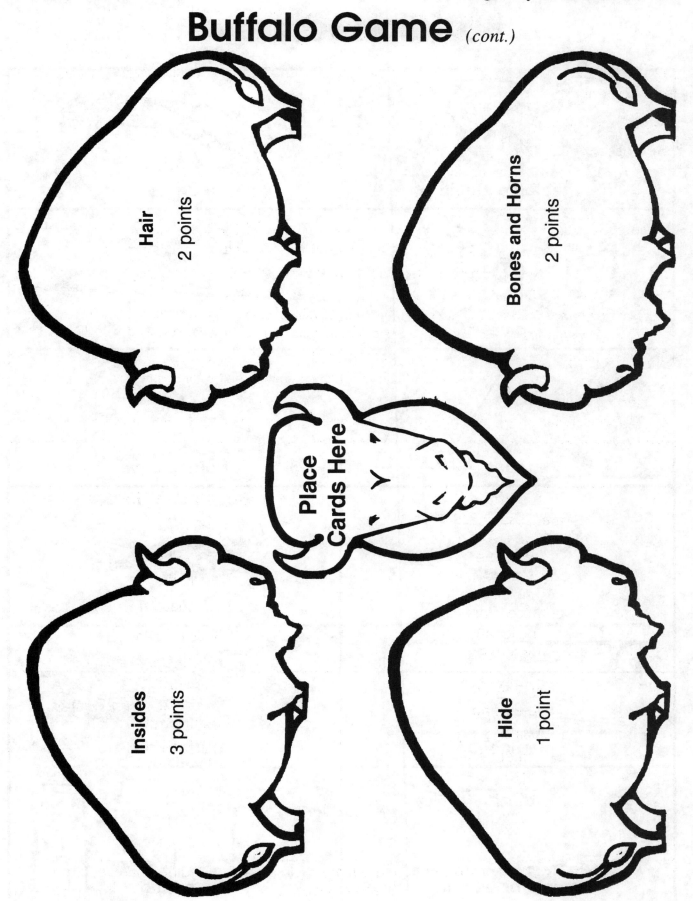

Hair
2 points

Bones and Horns
2 points

Place Cards Here

Insides
3 points

Hide
1 point

Buffalo Game *(cont.)*

medicine shield

bridle

dice

bow string

tepee

buffalo robe

bowl

buffalo chips

parfleche

buffalo rug

canvas for painting

clothing

Buffalo Game *(cont.)*

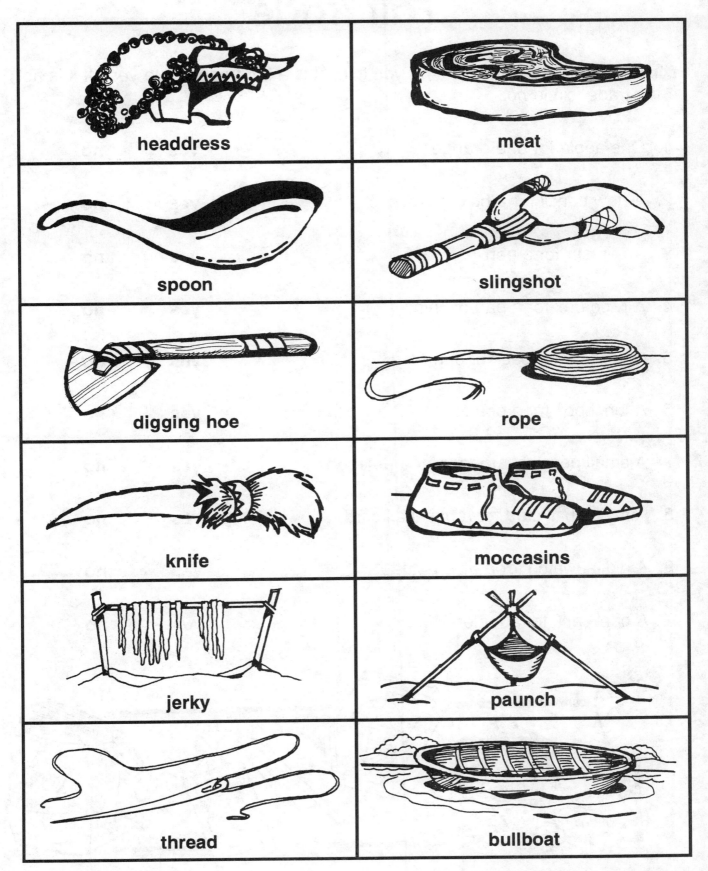

headdress	meat
spoon	slingshot
digging hoe	rope
knife	moccasins
jerky	paunch
thread	bullboat

Name_____

Fair Trade

Directions: Read each trade. If you think it is a fair trade, circle *yes*. If it is not a fair trade, circle *no*.

1. One apple for one orange	**yes**	**no**
2. A new pencil for a box of crayons	**yes**	**no**
3. An eraser for a pen	**yes**	**no**
4. A juice box for a bag of chips	**yes**	**no**
5. Cookies for a pack of gum	**yes**	**no**
6. A lunchbox for a poster	**yes**	**no**
7. A small pencil sharpener for a notebook	**yes**	**no**
8. A basketball card for a baseball card	**yes**	**no**
9. A digital watch for a glue bottle	**yes**	**no**
10. A backpack for a folder	**yes**	**no**

Community Ties

The following activity can be done individually or with a partner. Have the class research the Native Americans of their community (or those nearest to their community). They should investigate the lives of those from the past and those living today. Research on modern Native Americans has the added benefit of primary source interviews. Information about those from the past can be sought in the local library and through archival collections. To write their reports, the students can use page 76 as a guide.

Ideally, you can invite a Native American to be a guest speaker in your class. The form below can be used to write a thank you note to the guest speaker or to an individual who is interviewed.

As an extension following these activities, the class (or each child) can complete a chart which compares Little Gopher's community with the old and the present local communities.

··

Letter Form

_____

(date)

Dear _____,

_____

_____

_____

_____

_____

_____

_____

_____

_____,

_____

Name_____

Native Americans in My Community

Directions: Answer each question. Draw a picture or pictures to go with each answer. Use more paper if you need more room.

1. The Native American tribe in our community is the _____ _____.	2. Their houses were once made from _____. Today, the people of the tribe live in houses made of _____.
3. The people used to eat _____. Today, they eat _____.	4. The people used to wear _____. Today, they wear _____.

Amazing Grace: Summing It Up

Grace has a truly amazing imagination. Her love of books is the gateway to her creative genius. She believes in herself and is confident that she can do anything. When she begins to doubt herself, she has the loving support of both her mother and her grandmother.

Grace wants to play the part of Peter in the classroom production of *Peter Pan.* Her classmates try to discourage her by pointing out that because she is black and a girl, she cannot play the part of Peter.

Grace's grandmother takes her to see the ballet *Romeo and Juliet.* A beautiful black ballerina plays the leading role, one that is traditionally played by a white ballerina. Following the performance, Grace is inspired to practice for the part of Peter. She puts her heart and soul into the performance, and the class decides unanimously to give her the part of Peter Pan.

Getting to Know the Author

Mary Hoffman has written several books for children. Her first book, *White Magic,* was published in 1975. She has written over thirty-five books in all, including *My Grandma Has Black Hair* and *Nancy No Size.* Her interest in animals led her to write a series entitled *Animals in the Wild.* She is also a fellow of the London Zoological Society.

Mrs. Hoffman was born in Hampshire, England, and she currently lives in London with her husband and three daughters. She spends her time as a journalist and a freelance writer.

Getting to Know the Illustrator

Caroline Binch painted the colorful pictures for *Amazing Grace.* Ms. Binch lives in London, England, with her son. She makes a living by combining her creative talents. As a photographer, she is able to capture and share the beauty of the world with her camera. As a painter, she is able to recreate the images that she sees both in her environment and within her mind. *Amazing Grace* is the first book that she has illustrated.

Caroline Binch selected a medium of warm, rich, vibrant watercolors for *Amazing Grace.* The sheer beauty of the pictures gives life to the characters. Ms. Binch's pictures capture the spirit of the book, creating a more enjoyable story.

Getting Started

1. **Character Play:** As a class, brainstorm for the stories and characters read about in class this year. List them on the chalkboard. Have each child think of his/her favorite character and imagine being that character. Tell them that they are going to play a game wherein they will play the part of their favorite character for the rest of the class. The class will try to guess which character they are imitating. You may want to act out a character first to give the children an idea of what is expected.

   After completing this activity, explain to the children that they will be listening to a story about a girl named Grace who loves books and the characters in them. She spends a lot of time pretending to be those characters.

2. **History of Ghana:** Share with the students the following history of Ghana. If desired, the students can do further research as well.

   Ghana is located in Western Africa on the Atlantic Ocean's Gulf of Guinea, four hundred miles north of the equator. It is a small country, about the size of Montana. It was the first African nation south of the Sahara Desert to win independence from a colonial power. This occurred on March 6, 1957. However, the rich history of Ghana dates back for many thousands of years.

   Hunters from western Sudan drifted into what is now Ghana around the year 400. The Mali empire opened gold mines in Ghana shortly after the 12th century. In 1470, Portuguese traders arrived. During the 1500's, Britain, France, and the Netherlands made the first of many trading voyages. By the 1600's, the most important trade was the slave trade.

   The barbaric practice of slavery nearly decimated the population of Ghana. It is estimated that between 20 million and 60 million people were enslaved and brought to the Americas. Millions more were killed in the process, dying in the slave raids and in the holding dungeons built by the Portuguese.

   The Portuguese dungeons were small and cramped. One small cell, which could barely hold one hundred and fifty people, would be crowded with one thousand men for months at a time. One hundred and fifty women would be crowded into another cell, slightly smaller than the cell holding the men. The people were not given enough to eat, and there were no bathroom facilities. They were branded and sometimes shackled to a wall while being forced to stand in their own waste. Those who died or were driven insane were thrown into the ocean. The people who survived faced the long, deadly journey across the Atlantic Ocean on slave ships. These ships had the same type of inhumane conditions as the dungeons.

Getting Started *(cont.)*

As a small means of making amends for the past, Cape Coast Castle, which once held millions of slaves waiting for the slave ships, is now the West Africa Historical Museum.

By 1850, the British became the ruling colonial power of Ghana. In 1920, the first steps for freedom began as a group of Gold Coast Africans formed the Congress of British West Africa. In 1947, the Convention People's Party was formed. This group successfully gained Ghana's independence from Britain.

Today, the country's largest export is cocoa, and its major resources are gold, timber, and diamonds.

3. **History of Trinidad:** Share with the students the following history of Trinidad. If desired, the students can do further research as well.

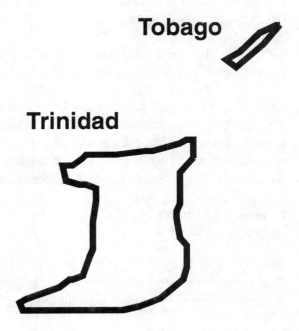

The island of Trinidad is the southernmost Caribbean island. It is located only seven miles off the coast of Venezuela. Its sister island, Tobago, is 21 miles northeast of Trinidad.

The first Trinidadians were Amerindians, part of the original people of the Americas, who settled the Caribbean islands centuries before Christopher Columbus "found" the island in 1498. Columbus named the island for the Holy Trinity, noting that it was "as green and lovely as the orchards of Valencia in March." The island was under Spanish rule for three centuries.

The Spanish had problems developing the island, so Spain encouraged the French to send settlers to Trinidad. However, in 1797, the British seized the island from Spain and began to import slaves from Africa. When slavery was abolished in 1830, the British brought in laborers from other parts of the world to work the sugarcane plantations. The majority of the laborers came from India and China; however, people from the Middle East and the Mediterranean also came to the island to seek their fortunes. It is often said of Trinidad, "In this country's veins runs the blood of half the world."

In 1956, Trinidad gained the right to self-govern. In 1962, Trinidad joined its neighbor, Tobago, and became independent. It became a republic in 1976, developing a democratic government. The Head of State is called President; however, all of the executive power is in the hands of the Prime Minister and the Cabinet.

People Are People

1. **Grace's Feelings:** Ask the children why they think Grace would make a good Peter Pan. List their responses on the board. Also, list the reasons given by Grace's classmates as to why she could not be Peter Pan. Discuss the validity of the reasons against her, being sure to mention Rosalie Wilkins from the story and Mary Martin, the definitive Broadway Peter Pan. Then, as a means to understanding Grace better and as a way to relate to Grace, have the students complete page 81.

2. **Real or Make-Believe?:** Discuss the difference between real and make-believe. Explain that when a person uses his or her imagination, that person can become anything he or she would like to be, whether real or fictional. Then, to further investigate the difference between real and make-believe, complete page 82.

3. **Great People and Characters from the Past:** Discuss some of the characters that Grace pretends to be. Read the additional information given below, and then complete page 83.

Joan of Arc: Jeanne d'Arc was a French peasant born in 1412. When she was thirteen years old, she began to hear voices telling her to liberate France from English rule. In 1429, she told King Charles VII about her calling. She led his troops in a battle at Orleans. In only eight days, Joan was victorious. However, in 1431, a church court tricked her into an admission of heresy and witchcraft. She was burned at the stake on May 30, 1431.

Anansi the Spider: This fictional folk hero appears in various tales from West Africa. Anansi is known for causing mischief. He is humorous yet wise, and he triumphs over larger opponents.

The Gates of Troy: In Homer's *Iliad* and *Odyssey,* a large wooden horse filled with Greek soldiers is left at the gates of Troy. The Greek soldiers leap from the horse once it is wheeled into the city. A battle is waged, leaving the Greeks victorious.

Hiawatha: Hiawatha was an Iroquois and a member of the Mohawk tribe. Because the five Iroquois tribes were constantly fighting, he created a new form of government called the Five Nations Iroquois League, an early American model of government similar to the United Nations. Hiawatha's efforts led to peace among the tribes.

Mowgli: In *The Jungle Book* by Rudyard Kipling, a baby boy named Mowgli is left in the jungle. He is raised and protected by the animals there.

Aladdin: In *Aladdin and the Magic Lamp,* the title character finds a lamp with a genie inside. The genie promises to obey the young boy and grant him three wishes.

Peter Pan: Peter Pan is the title character in a book by J.M. Barrie. He leads a group of young boys like himself who never want to grow up.

Juliet: *Romeo and Juliet* is a famous play by William Shakespeare. It tells the story of a teenage boy and girl from two feuding families who fall in love, secretly marry, and then die tragically.

Name_____

Grace's Feelings

Directions: Color the face that matches how you think Grace feels.

1. Nana tells Grace a story.

2. The teacher tells the class they are going to perform *Peter Pan*.

3. Raj says Grace cannot be Peter Pan because she is a girl.

4. Natalie says Grace cannot be Peter Pan because he is not black.

5. Grace tells her mother what the children said to her in school.

6. Grace and Nana go to the ballet.

7. Grace auditions for Peter Pan.

8. Grace wins the part of Peter Pan.

9. Grace performs in the play.

10. Nana watches Grace in the play.

Name_____

Real or Make-Believe?

Directions: Circle *real* if the person is real and *make-believe* if the person is make-believe.

1. Peter Pan	**real**	**make-believe**
2. Joan of Arc	**real**	**make-believe**
3. Cinderella	**real**	**make-believe**
4. Martin Luther King, Jr.	**real**	**make-believe**
5. Harriet Tubman	**real**	**make-believe**
6. Mowgli	**real**	**make-believe**
7. Mary McLeod Bethune	**real**	**make-believe**
8. Nelson Mandela	**real**	**make-believe**
9. Hiawatha	**real**	**make-believe**
10. Anansi the Spider	**real**	**make-believe**
11. George Washington	**real**	**make-believe**
12. Aladdin	**real**	**make-believe**
13. Clara Barton	**real**	**make-believe**
14. Malcolm X	**real**	**make-believe**
15. Goldilocks	**real**	**make-believe**

Name_____

Great People from the Past

Directions: Read each paragraph. Circle the correct answer after each.

Joan of Arc

Joan of Arc lived in France a long time ago. When her country was in a war with England, she led an army. She was a very brave young woman. In eight days, her army won back the city of Orleans, and she came to be called the Maid of Orleans. Joan of Arc is a national heroine.

1. Joan of Arc lived in_____.
   - A. America
   - B. France
   - C. New Orleans

2. Joan of Arc led _____.
   - A. a parade
   - B. a football team
   - C. an army

3. Joan of Arc is _____.
   - A. a heroine
   - B. a villain
   - C. a hero

Hiawatha

Hiawatha was a Mohawk Indian. He wanted peace for all Iroquois tribes, so he talked to the tribes about getting along. He asked each tribe to promise not to fight each other. They promised to live peacefully. With Hiawatha's help, they formed the Five Nation Iroquois League. The League is like the United Nations.

1. Hiawatha was a (an) _____ Indian.
   - A. Plains
   - B. Mohawk
   - C. Apache

2. Hiawatha wanted the tribes to stop _____.
   - A. fighting
   - B. eating
   - C. fishing

3. Hiawatha formed the _____.
   - A. United Nations
   - B. Mohawk tribe
   - C. Five Nation Iroquois League

Socializing Skills: Breaking Down Stereotypes

The purpose of these activities is to teach the students how to break down stereotypes and to follow their dreams. The activities will help the students to understand what a stereotype is and to recognize that stereotypes are misleading at best. They will also encourage the students to think about their own dreams for the future and enable them to make a plan to fulfill those dreams.

1. **Breaking Down Stereotypes**: Review with the children some of the things Grace is told as to why she cannot be Peter Pan. Then, tell them that these statements are based on stereotypes (judgments based on opinion, partial information, or misinformation, not fact).

   Ask the children if they have heard of the stereotypes that say girls should not play with cars, and boys should not play with dolls. Explain that some girls may not like to play with cars, but other girls do. The same holds true for boys and dolls.

   Have the students give examples of stereotypes they have heard. Here is a list of some common ones.
   - *Men cannot cook.*
   - *Women cannot drive.*
   - *Only girls wear pink.*
   - *Boys do not cry.*
   - *Girls cannot play sports.*
   - *Boys do not like dance lessons.*

   List these stereotypes on the chalkboard along with any others that your students remember. Then, across from each stereotype, write why it is not true. For example, many men enjoy dancing and want to improve their dance skills, and others, such as gymnasts, football players, and ice skaters, may take lessons to improve their flexibility.

   Provide each child with a piece of paper. They can write and draw a stereotype on half the paper, and then on the other half, draw and write a statement that shows the stereotype to be incorrect.

   Do pages 85 and 86 as practice in identifying stereotypes.

2. **A Dream for Me!:** This activity will encourage the children to follow their dreams, regardless of stereotypes. Begin the lesson by listing on the board some careers that have been linked to a gender stereotype (such as police officer, doctor, secretary, and so forth). Discuss the stereotypes and why they are incorrect. Explain that anybody can do these jobs if he/she is qualified.

   Discuss the type of training a person will need for each career. Then pass out page 87. Use this page to serve as a motivator for the students. Have them cut out and color the bookmark as a reminder of their ability to achieve their dreams.

   Students may also enjoy the song, "Jump Shamador." A source for this song can be found on page 141. The song allows the students to sing about the type of career they wish to pursue one day, while at the same time loudly declaring that they can do it.

3. **Additional Literature:** As an extension, read either *William's Doll* or *Oliver Button Is a Sissy*. (See the bibliography, page 141.)

Name_____

Breaking Down Stereotypes

Directions: Read each sentence. If the sentence is a stereotype, cross it out.

1. Women are the best cooks.

2. All doctors should be men, and nurses should be women.

3. It is all right for boys and girls to cry.

4. Boys do not wear pink.

5. Some good cooks are men.

6. Pretty women are not smart.

7. Some people cannot dance well.

8. Boys do not like to read.

9. Girls dislike math.

10. Boys are the best baseball players.

Name_____

Unscrambling Stereotypes

Directions: Unscramble the words to form sentences that break common stereotypes.

1. drivers men women both good be can and

   _____

2. take girls lessons and boys can dance

   _____

3. baseball play girls can boys and well

   _____

4. can blue anybody wear

   _____

5. they boys can and are when girls cry sad

   _____

6. dolls play trucks anybody can with cars and

   _____

7. and pink boys girls wear can

   _____

8. women good some are men and cooks

   _____

9. be men doctors women can and

   _____

10. become a anyone can secretary

    _____

Name_____

A Dream for Me!

Directions: Fill in all the blanks. Cut out and color the bookmark at the bottom of the page.

I can become a _____

Here are two things I can do now to make my dream come true.

Here are two things I can do when I am older to make my dream come true.

If I believe it ...   I will achieve it.

Getting from Here to There

These geography lessons focus on Ghana, Trinidad, and the United States. To begin the lessons, it will be helpful to review the concept of stereotyping. Explain to the students that people have been stereotyping for thousands of years.

1. **Putting It All Together:** In *Amazing Grace,* Nana mentions that she is from Trinidad. From the beginning of the 18th century, Africans were brought as slaves to Trinidad. Most came from west Africa, in the area now known as Ghana.

   Ask the children what they think slavery is. Listen to their responses. Explain that slavery around the world has involved many different races of people. The most common form of slavery in the United States involved Africans being enslaved by European Americans.

   Slavery is usually a direct result of stereotypes. In the United States, the following stereotypes helped to promote slavery. Break them down with the students.

   Africans are not humans.

   Africans are strong and suited for hard work.

   Africans prefer being cared for by a master.

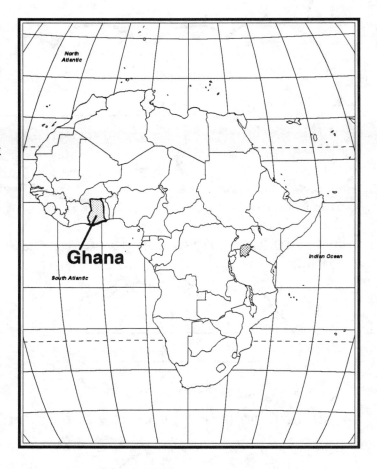

Ghana

Now, pass out page 90. Show the children Ghana. Explain that Africans were brought by slave ships to Trinidad to work on the sugar plantations. Some Africans went directly to the United States while others went to various Caribbean islands.

Explain that the Africans were treated very poorly. Many never made it to the islands or to North America because of the conditions on the slave ships. Once on land, the slaves were still made to live under harsh conditions. They had poorly constructed homes, few articles of clothing, and little nutritional food to eat. But most importantly, they had no freedom.

The colors green, black, and red will be used on page 90 because they are symbols for African American people. Green represents the wealth of Africa. Red is for the struggle and the blood shed by African Americans. Black is for the people.

To complete page 90, the students will need the three colors, scissors, and glue.

Getting from Here to There *(cont.)*

2. **Using Symbols:** Page 91 compares the climates of Ghana, Trinidad, and the United States. In Trinidad, the wet season is from June through December. It rains virtually everyday. In Ghana, there are only two seasons: wet and dry. From March through July is the wet season. August is a dry month, and then September through November is another rainy season. From December until February it is dry and windy. Ghana is sometimes subject to droughts where there is very little rainfall.

   To complete page 91, you will need to discuss the climate of your community. Have the children bring in weather forecasts from your area. Do some research to determine typical weather patterns. Use this information and the information from the paragraph above to complete the chart.

   You can also create a weather prediction chart for Trinidad and Ghana. Have the children guess what the weather is like or what the temperature is in Trinidad and Ghana, and then have them look in magazines or national newspapers to find out what the weather is really like there.

3. **Big Deals:** Page 92 will teach the children about large landforms in Trinidad, the United States, and Ghana.

   Lake Brea is the largest tar pit in the world, and it is located in the southeastern portion of Trinidad. It is about 200 feet (60 meters) deep. The asphalt in it is so thick that trucks can be driven over it. The natural asphalt from Lake Brea is exported all over the world to pave streets.

   The Grand Canyon is a gorge in northwestern Arizona that was carved by the Colorado River. It is a colorful, enormous piece of natural beauty. It is 217 miles (349 km) long, stretching from the Little Colorado River to Lake Mead. Some parts of the canyon are a mile (1.6 km) deep and from four to eighteen miles (6.5 to 29 km) wide. Over a billion years of erosion have created this enormous gorge, the largest in the United States.

   Lake Volta is one of the largest manmade lakes in the world. It is located in Ghana, and it covers 3,275 square miles (8,482 square kilometers). It is fed by the Volta River. When the Akosombo Dam project was completed in 1965, Lake Volta was created as a reservoir behind the dam. The Akosombo hydroelectric dam provides the entire country with electricity.

4. **Port of Spain, Trinidad:** Page 93 will be used to improve map reading skills and to learn more about the island of Trinidad. You can also take this opportunity to do some research on Carnival. See page 94 for more information.

Putting It All Together

Name _____

The United States

Africa

**Trinidad
and
Tobago**

Directions:

1. Color Africa green. Green is for the wealth of the continent.

2. Color the United States red. Red is for the struggles African Americans have overcome.

3. Color Trinidad and Tobago black. Black is for the people.

4. Glue a slave ship between Africa and Trinidad. Africans arrived in Trinidad as slaves.

5. Glue a slave ship between Africa and the United States. Africans came to the U.S.A. as slaves.

6. Glue the plane between Trinidad and the U.S.A. People come to the U.S.A. from Trinidad as free people.

Name _____

Using Symbols

Directions: Use these symbols to fill in the chart.

hot    *wet*    *snowy*

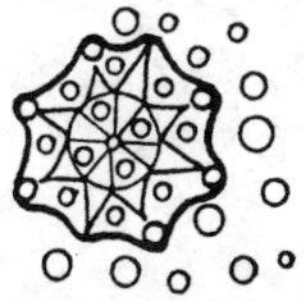

Ghana

Jan.	Feb.	Mar.	Apr.	May	June	July	Aug.	Sept.	Oct.	Nov.	Dec.

March through July are wet months.
August is dry and hot.
September through November is rainy.
From December through February it is hot, dry, and windy.

Trinidad

Jan.	Feb.	Mar.	Apr.	May	June	July	Aug.	Sept.	Oct.	Nov.	Dec.

From June through December it rains almost every day.
The rest of the year is sunny and warm.

Your City

Jan.	Feb.	Mar.	Apr.	May	June	July	Aug.	Sept.	Oct.	Nov.	Dec.

Name_____

Big Deals

Directions: Trace the dotted lines. Color each picture.

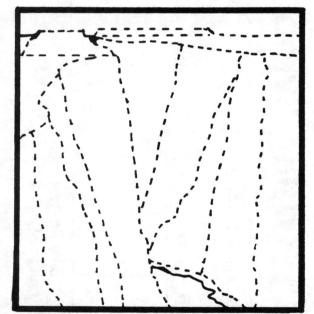

Trinidad

Lake Brea is the largest tar pit in the world. It produces asphalt naturally.

United States

The Grand Canyon is a giant gorge in Arizona. It extends for 217 miles (349 km).

Akosombo Dam

Ghana

Lake Volta is one of the largest manmade lakes in the world. It extends for 250 miles (402 km) behind Akosombo Dam.

Name_____

Port of Spain, Trinidad

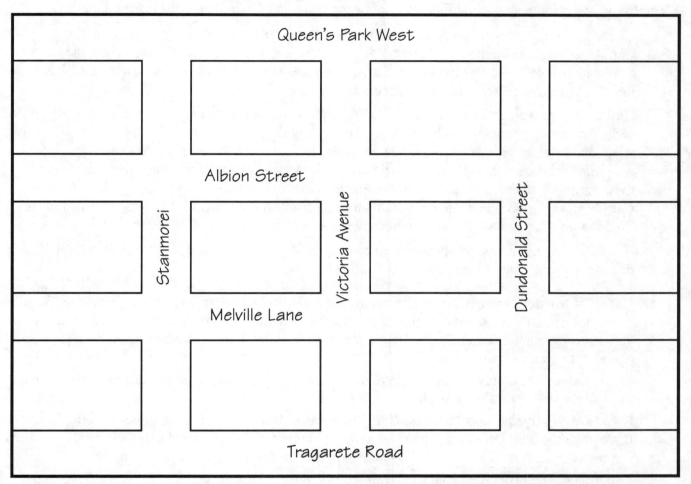

Queen's Park West

Albion Street

Stanmorei

Victoria Avenue

Dundonald Street

Melville Lane

Tragarete Road

Directions: Use a crayon to follow the route of the Carnival dancers.

1. Begin at Tragarete Road and Victoria Avenue.

2. Go one block north.

3. Go one block west.

4. Go two blocks north.

5. Go one block east.

6. Go two blocks south.

7. Go one block east.

8. Go one block south.

9. Where do you arrive? _____

Experiencing the Culture

The following activities will highlight aspects of the cultures of Trinidad, Tobago, and Ghana.

1. **Carnival:** African and French cultures unite to create Carnival, the largest festival in the Caribbean Islands. Carnival is based in art, religion, and politics. The French aristocracy customarily celebrated Carnival from Christmas until Ash Wednesday. The celebration was linked to a Roman Catholic festival which occurs before Lent.

   During the festival, French planters disguised themselves and paraded down the streets. When the 1863 American emancipation bill was passed, freeing the slaves, some Africans in America began an annual celebration. They dressed in costumes and imitated the French. Yet, each year the government chose to make it more difficult for the Africans to celebrate their freedom. Therefore, they combined their celebration with the French Carnival. As time has passed, the African-Caribbean culture has become the dominant participant in the festival. Likewise, the islands of Trinidad and Tobago are the dominant celebrants of Carnival in the Caribbean.

   If possible, bring in a guest speaker who has attended Carnival festivities, or if you are lucky, one or more of your students will have firsthand experience.

2. **Carnival Music:** During Carnival, the sound of the steel bands can be heard everywhere. These drums are the only musical instruments invented during this century, aside from electronic variations on other older designs. They are made from metal oil cans which have been fired and pounded to create various tones.

   Calypso music also plays a major role in the celebration. You can look for calypso music to play in your classroom. Calypso is played in 2-3 time.

   Page 96 gives instructions for constructing musical instruments similar to those used in Carnival. Encourage the children to play their instruments along with the recorded calypso music. Students can then make Carnival masks and parade and perform for the rest of the school.

3. **Language:** The official language of Trinidad is English. However, some slang is unique to the culture.

Bacchanal:	rowdy behavior
Beat pan:	play the steel band
Commesse:	confusion
Free up:	relax
Jump up:	dance
Lime:	spend time talking and laughing
Maco:	a person who is noisy
Ol' talk:	empty chatter

   Individual students or groups can write a story and incorporate some of these slang terms into it. Choose a topic that is related to Carnival. Perhaps you might have the children imagine how it would feel to participate in Carnival. They can write about their ideas.

Experiencing the Culture *(cont.)*

4. **Kente Cloth and Adinkra:** *Kente,* the original royal fabric of Ghana, can be studied on pages 97-98. The bright red, gold, blue, and green patterns represent a rich heritage dating back to the eleventh century. Each pattern's name usually refers to a proverb.

   Traditionally, this fabric was wrapped toga-style around a man. Women wore two identical cloths. One was worn as a shawl. Modern adaptations of the original Kente Cloth can be found on T-shirts, hats, and buttons. If possible, bring in some to show your students. Have them complete page 98 to learn more about Kente Cloth.

   You can also encourage your students to create their own designs. Divide students into cooperative groups of four. Each group will select two or three colors to use in its design. Have two of the children create a design using straight lines, and have the other two students create a design that uses shapes. Suggest that they keep the design simple, like the ones in the original Kente Cloths. Provide the children with squares of paper that are 3 x 3 inches (8 x 8 cm). Have them color their patterns onto the paper. Glue them onto a piece of construction paper that is 12 x 15 inches (30 x 38 cm). Glue the line pattern next to the shape pattern.

   Adinkra comes from the Akan people of Ghana. Long ago, they were ruled by their beloved king, Adinkira. To please him, his servants created the most beautiful cloth imaginable. Special symbols were printed on the cloth, each with its own meaning. The cloth was made into a robe for the king. However, when King Adinkira died in battle against the Ashanti, the cloth was taken by his foes. The Ashanti named the cloth after the dead king. The Akan people wore the Adinkra symbols at his funeral. As time passed, the people continued to use such cloth in the funerals of their dead loved ones, so that today it is traditionally worn after someone dies. The colors of the cloth are shades of red, indigo, and burnt orange.

   To study Adinkra, use page 97.

5. **Day Names:** Day names are a wonderful way to personalize African tradition. See page 99 for details.

6. **____'s Book of Proverbs:** Each of the proverbs on page 100 is from the Ashanti people of Ghana. Discuss with your students what they mean. Then, illustrate them and form a mini-book.

   After completing the proverb book, have the children think of other proverbs they have heard. (Prompt younger students with the first few words of some proverbs.) Make a list of these proverbs and discuss each one. Then assign each child a proverb to illustrate, and put them all together in a class book.

7. **African-American Recipes:** Delicious and fun recipes can be found on page 101. Prepare them as a class, and then enjoy them while making Kente cloth patterns.

8. **Games from Africa and Trinidad:** Students will enjoy playing the games included on page 102. All they require is some imagination and observation.

9. **Traveling with Grace Game:** The board game found on pages 103-105 will test the students' knowledge of Ghana, Trinidad, and the U.S..

Carnival Music

How to Make a Drum

Materials:

- coffee can with plastic lid
- construction paper
- glitter
- glue or tape
- scissors

Directions:

1. Cut the paper so that it fits around the can, and glue it in place.

2. Draw designs with glue on the paper.

3. Sprinkle glitter over the wet glue and let the drum dry.

4. Put the lid on the can. Strike either end of the drum with one of the drumsticks suggested below.

Drumsticks:

Use one, some, or all of the following:

- pencil with a large eraser on the end
- pencil with a metal nut on the end
- coat hanger section with a cork on the end
- dowel with a wooden bead on the end

How to Make a Shaker

Materials:

- two paper plates
- hole punch
- yarn
- crayons
- dry macaroni, beans, or peas

Directions:

1. Place the plates on top of each other.

2. Make holes ½ inch (1 cm) apart around the plate edges. Be sure to punch holes in both plates at the same time.

3. Decorate the outside of each plate.

4. Put 2 tablespoons (30 mL) of the dry food in one of the plates.

5. To sew the plates together, tape one end of the yarn to form a point. This will make the sewing easier.

6. Place the plates on top of each other and sew them together by going around from the bottom up on every stitch.

7. After sewing around the plates, tie knots in the two loose pieces of yarn and trim the excess.

Name_____

Kente Cloth and Adinkra

Directions: Read each paragraph. Then below it, circle the "T" after each true statement or "F" after each false statement.

Kente Cloth

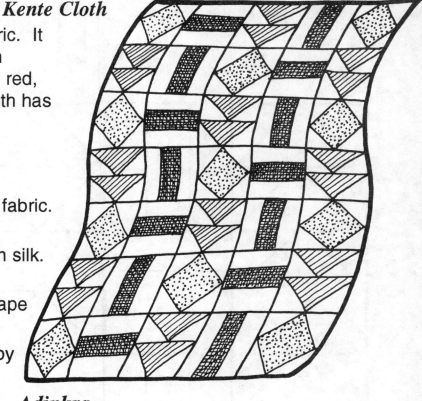

Kente Cloth was once a royal fabric. It is made from cotton, silk, or rayon fibers. The colors of the cloth are red, blue, yellow, and green. Each cloth has a pattern of lines or shapes.

1. Pink is a color in Kente Cloth.
   T   F

2. Kente Cloth was once a royal fabric.
   T   F

3. Kente Cloth can be made from silk.
   T   F

4. Each cloth is made only of shape patterns.   **T   F**

5. Kente Cloth used to be worn by peasants.   **T   F**

Adinkra

Adinkra is a fabric from Ghana, named for a beloved king from long ago. It is traditionally worn after somebody dies. Tree bark and the roots of plants are used to make the dye for the fabric. Adinkra symbols are hand stamped onto the fabric. The colors of Adinkra are soothing shades of red, indigo blue, and burnt orange.

1. Adinkra symbols are stamped onto the fabric.   **T   F**

2. Adinkra is from Trinidad.   **T   F**

3. Indigo blue is a color used in Adinkra fabric.   **T   F**

4. Adinkra is named for a country.   **T   F**

5. Adinkra is traditionally worn after a death.   **T   F**

Name_____

Color the Kente Cloth

Directions: Color all ⬜△ green. Color all ◇ red. Color all ▭ yellow. Color all ▯ blue. Leave everywhere else white.

Day Names

When a child is born, it is given a "day" name along with a family name. If the child is Christian, a Christian name is also given. The following chart lists the days of the week and the name given to a girl or boy born on each day.

Day	Boy Name	Girl Name	Meaning (Child of...)
Sunday	Kwesi	Akosua	the sun
Monday	Kwadwo	Adwoa	peace
Tuesday	Kwabena	Abena	fire
Wednesday	Kwaku	Akua	fame
Thursday	Yaw	Yaa	strength
Friday	Kofi	Afua	growth
Saturday	Kwame	Amma	most ancient

After each child has found his/her day name and its meaning (students may first need to ask their parents on which day of the week they were born), have them each prepare a name wall-hanging.

Bring a baby name book to school and allow the children to look up the meaning and origin of their first names. Each child will then need crayons, a piece of 12 x 18 inch (30 x 45 cm) construction paper, a clothes hanger, and glue. Fold over 1 inch (2.5 cm) of the top of the paper. Make sure the students know that this fold is the top of their wall hanging.

On the paper, have each student write his/her name, its meaning and origin, and his/her day name and meaning. The children can then illustrate their wall hangings according to the name meanings. They may also want to include their birth dates and anything else they feel makes them unique.

After decorating the paper, place the folded edge over the hanger and glue the edge to the back of the paper. Display these in the classroom, and then send them home with the students.

_____'s Book of

Proverbs

Every man carries his own mark.

Two small antelope can beat one big one.

There is no medicine to cure hatred.

African-American Recipes

Peanut Punch

Ingredients:

- ½ cup (125 mL) smooth peanut butter
- 3 cups (750 mL) cold milk
- 4 tablespoons (60 mL) sugar
- dash of cinnamon
- dash of nutmeg

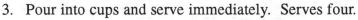

Directions:

1. Measure each ingredient and pour them together into a blender.

2. Set the blender to a high speed and blend for 30 seconds. The punch should look thick and foamy.

3. Pour into cups and serve immediately. Serves four.

Betty's Browned-down Chicken

Ingredients:

- 3 pounds (1,500 g) chicken
- 1 medium onion (sliced)
- 1 teaspoon (5 mL) salt
- 1 teaspoon (5 mL) thyme
- 1 tablespoon (15 mL) sugar
- ½ cup (125 mL) vegetable oil
- 2 cloves garlic (crushed)
- 1 red chili (seeded and chopped)
- ½ teaspoon (2.5 mL) black pepper
- dash of ginger
- 2 tablespoons (30 mL) apple cider vinegar

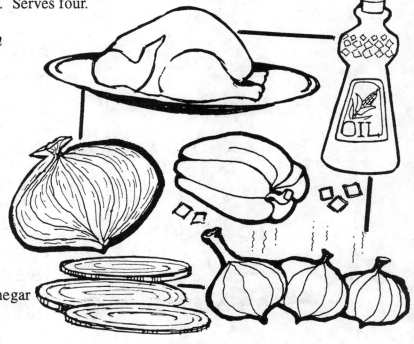

Directions:

1. Wash the chicken and rub with garlic.

2. Place the chicken in a large bowl and add onions, salt, thyme, chili, pepper, and ginger.

3. Pour vinegar over the chicken, cover tightly, and refrigerate overnight.

4. In a large frying pan, combine the sugar and oil.

5. Cook over a medium heat, stirring constantly, until the sugar has dissolved. This will take about four to five minutes.

6. Scrape the onions off the chicken. Save the onions and the vinegar mixture.

7. Cut chicken into pieces. Brown a few pieces at a time, browning all sides evenly before removing them from the pan.

8. Return the browned chicken to the pan, add the onions and vinegar mixture, and add enough water to almost cover the chicken.

9. Cover and cook over a medium heat for 30 minutes or until the chicken is tender. Save the meat juices to use as a gravy over rice. Serves four to six.

Games from Africa and Trinidad

The following games are similar to some of the games that western children play.

Ampe

Ampe is a jumping game from Ghana. To play, the children are divided into two teams. One child is "It." That child chooses somebody from the opposing team to challenge. The two children jump in unison three times. When they land from the third jump, they each stick out one foot. If the challenger does not have the same foot out as the person who is "It," the challenger loses. If the challenger matches, then he or she wins. The winner chooses somebody from the other team to challenge.

Kye, Kye, Kule

Kye, Kye, Kule (pronounced *chee, chee, koo-lay*) are nonsense words. To play the game, one person stands in the middle while the rest of the class makes a ring around him or her. The leader sings out, "Kye, kye, kule," and then strikes a pose. The rest of the class echoes back the words and then strikes the same pose. The leader sings out and poses two more times. After the third pose, the leader falls on the ground. The rest of the players fall to the ground as well. Then, suddenly the leader jumps up and tries to tag another child. The children can run only after the leader has started running. The child who is tagged becomes "It," and the game starts all over again.

There's a Brown Girl in the Ring

There's a Brown Girl in the Ring is a game from Trinidad. It is similar to Kye, Kye, Kule. One child stands in the middle, and the others hold hands to form a ring around her. As the first verse is sung, the children holding hands walk in a circle. As the second verse is sung, the child in the middle strikes a pose and the others copy the pose. During the third verse, the child in the middle selects another child to take her place in the center. Then the game starts all over again. You may also play the game with a boy in the center by calling it "There's a Brown Boy in the Ring."

The words and music for this game can be found in *Shake It to the One That You Love the Best: Play Songs and Lullabies from Black Musical Traditions*. (See the bibliography.)

Traveling with Grace Game

Materials: answer card (page 103), 12 playing cards (page 104), gameboard (page 105), markers for play, a brad, and the spinner arrow (page 103)

Directions for Preparing the Game:
1. Color and laminate the gameboard.
2. Color, laminate, and cut out the cards.
3. Cut out and laminate the answer card.
4. Cut out and laminate the spinner arrow. Use the brad to attach the center of the arrow to the center of the spinner on the gameboard. (Do not affix the brad too tightly, or the arrow will not spin.)

Directions for Play:
1. Place the cards face down in a pile on the gameboard. Place all markers on *start*.
2. Decide who will pick first. (Play in birthday order, alphabetically by first name, or any other neutral determinant.)
3. The first player spins the arrow and moves. If he/she lands on a question mark, that player chooses a card from the pile and answers the question. Check the answer against the answer card. If the player has answered correctly, he/she moves ahead two spaces. If the player has answered incorrectly, he/she moves back one space.
4. The winner is the first person to reach the finish line.

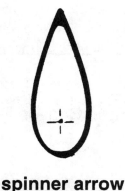

spinner arrow

Answer Card
- A. Trinidad
- B. Ghana
- C. United States
- D. United States
- E. Ghana
- F. Trinidad
- G. The United States
- H. Ghana
- I. Trinidad
- J. Trinidad
- K. Ghana
- L. United States

Traveling with Grace Game *(cont.)*

A. This country is an island.	B. This country is in Africa.
C. This country is in North America.	D. The colors of the national flag are red, white, and blue.
E. The colors of the national flag are red, yellow, and green.	F. This country celebrates Carnival.
G. This country celebrates the Fourth of July.	H. Kente Cloth comes from this country.
I. Red, white, and black are the colors of this country's flag.	J. Lake Brea is in this country.
K. Lake Volta is in this country.	L. The Grand Canyon is in this country.

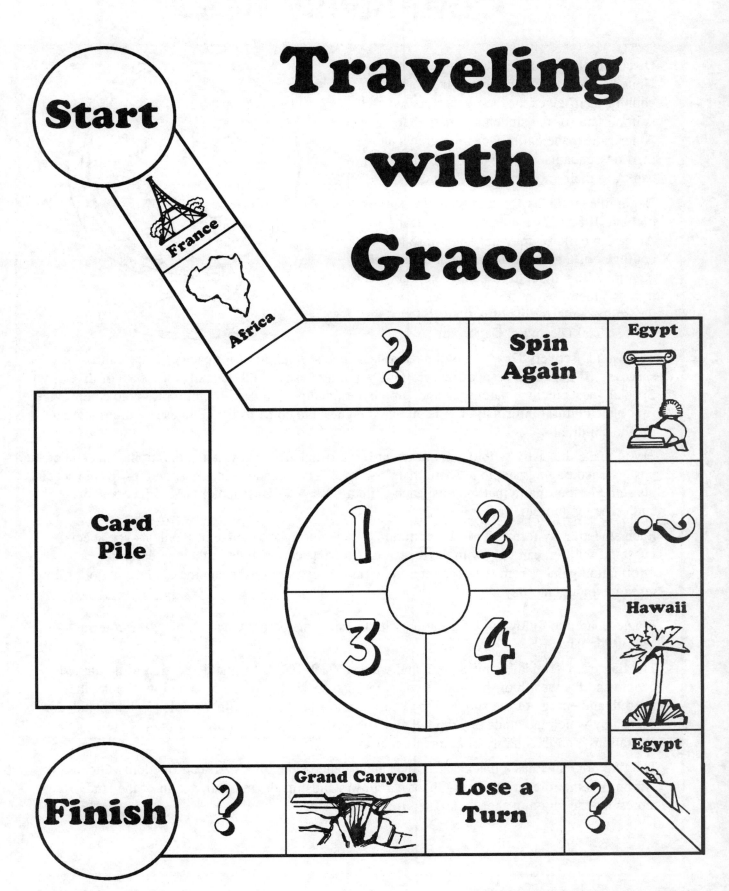

Traveling with Grace

Start

France

Africa

?

Spin Again

Egypt

Card Pile

1 2 3 4

Hawaii

Egypt

Finish

?

Grand Canyon

Lose a Turn

?

Community Ties

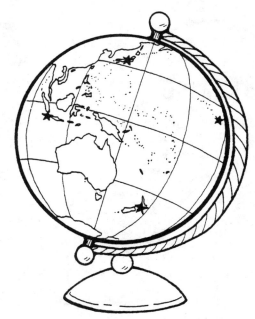

1. **Discovery Day:** All people living in the United States have either come from another country themselves, or their ancestors have. It is important for the students to note that America is made entirely of immigrants and their descendants. Even Native Americans can trace their ancestry to other lands.

   Begin this lesson by sending home the survey on page 108. Please note, many African-American children may only be aware of the continent of their ancestry and not the specific nation. Allow them to research a country that interests them. After reviewing the surveys, determine a master list of nations to focus on for a special Discovery Day event.

   To host a Discovery Day, you will need at least one special guest for each country/culture of your surveys. (If the cultural ancestries are few, you may wish to add others for the sake of diversity.) Special guests include parents, school employees, and people in the community who can provide first-hand cultural information. Encourage the guests to come to the class as resources and aids for the children.

   Try to make this activity into a major event for the students. They can make invitations and create posters encouraging people to share their histories. They can also make name tags for the special guests. For their participation, give each child a Discovery Day book mark. Videotape or audiotape the presentations.

   Each student may research his/her cultural heritage during the course of the day. The special guests, if willing, can help with the research. Students can include in their research the information gained from the guest presentations. They themselves can make presentations of their research on another day.

2. **Flags:** Share the following information with the students before they complete the coloring activity on page 109.

   The flag from Trinidad is black, red, and white. Black stands for the dedication of the united people and the wealth of the land. Red represents the vitality of the land and its people, the warmth and energy of the sun, and the courage and friendliness of the people. White stands for the sea by which the lands of Trinidad and Tobago are bound, the purity of the people's aspirations, and the quality of all men under the sun.

   The flag of Ghana has a black star in the center which symbolizes African freedom. Green symbolizes the forest regions of Ghana. Yellow stands for the mineral wealth of the land. Red represents the blood of those who died for independence.

Community Ties *(cont.)*

The flag of the United States has fifty stars representing the fifty states. There are thirteen stripes, seven red and six white. The stripes represent the thirteen original colonies. Red is for hardiness and courage. White represents purity and innocence. Blue is for vigilance, perseverance, and justice.

3. **People at Work:** Page 110 will give the students an opportunity to practice graph making and reading skills. It will also teach about the kinds of jobs the people in Ghana and Trinidad have.

4. **Bulletin Board:** It is interesting to note that the United States, Trinidad, and Ghana all have culturally diverse societies. Share the following information with the students.

More than fifty different ethnic groups live in Ghana. Each ethnic group has its own language, dialect, traditions, and beliefs. The largest ethnic group is the Akan which makes up 44% of the population. Other large ethnic groups are Asante, Mossi-Dagomba, Ewe, Ga-Adangme, and the Gurma.

The first people of Trinidad were Amerindians. These original people of the Americas settled the Caribbean islands centuries before Columbus set sail. A very small number of them still live in Trinidad today. Descendants of people from Africa, Spain, France, the Middle East, the Mediterranean, China, and India now live on the island.

Citizens of the United States hail from Africa, Asia, Europe, South America, North America—everywhere. Everyone in the United States can trace their ancestry to another country or continent.

Using this information combined with the results of Discovery Day, devise a bulletin board that displays the varying backgrounds of the people in these countries and/or in your classroom. Put a map of each country on the board. Use paper dolls in a rainbow of colors to represents the many cultures. Allow the students to make the dolls for the bulletin board.

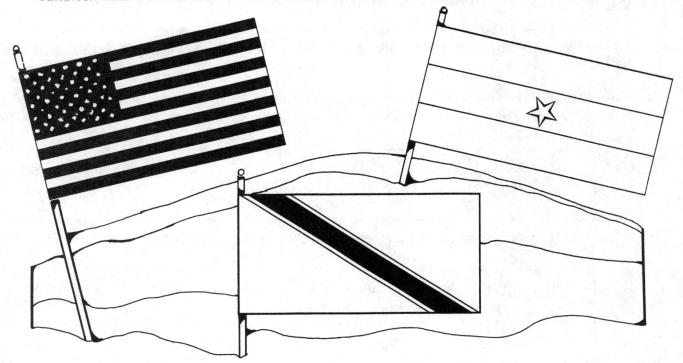

Discovery Day Survey for Parents

Dear Parents and Guardians,

We are preparing for a Discovery Day in our classroom. The focus of the day will be research into the cultures of our ancestries. We would like your help. Please answer the questions below and return the survey to school with your child. If you can help us, please list your phone number so that I may call you to make arrangements. Our Discovery Day is scheduled for _____ .

Thank you,

_____

Name_____

Phone Number _____

1. What is the national origin of your family name or names?

   _____

2. From what country or countries did your ancestors come?

   _____

3. If you do not know the country, give the continent or a nation with whose cultural identity you feel an affinity.

   _____

4. Are you familiar with the culture or cultures of your ancestors?

   _____

5. Do you have pictures of people currently living in the country or countries of your ancestry?

   _____

6. Do you have music or artwork from your culture or cultures that you would like to share with our class?

   _____

7. Do you know how to cook food from your culture or cultures?

   _____

8. Do you have books (reference, travel, etc.) from your culture or cultures that you would be willing to share with the class?

   _____

9. Would you be willing to work with a group of students on Discovery Day?

   _____

10. Would you be willing to make a presentation about your culture or cultures on Discovery Day?

    _____

Name_____

Flags of Trinidad, Ghana, and the United States

Directions: Unscramble the words. Color each flag.

United States

blue	red
	white
	red
	white
	red
	white
	red
white
red
white
red
white
red

courage = dre _____

purity = htwei _____

justice = uble _____

Ghana

| red |
| black ——— ☆   gold |
| green |

blood = erd _____

minerals = ogld _____

forests = rnege _____

earth = abckl _____

water = ehiwt _____

fire = der _____

Trinidad

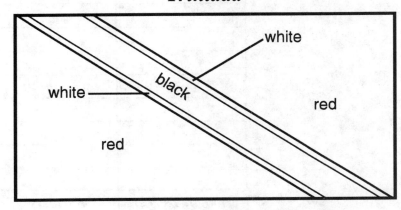

Name_____

People at Work in Trinidad and Ghana

1. Deborah lives in Port of Spain. She asked everybody on her block where they work. Use the information she got to complete Deborah's chart.

   - Three people work on farms.
   - Eight people work in hotels.
   - Four people build things.

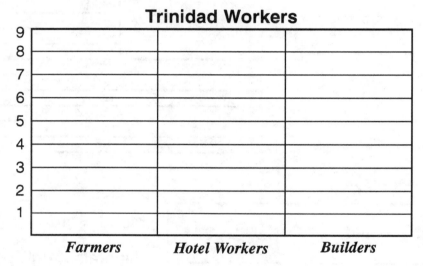

Trinidad Workers

Farmers   *Hotel Workers*   *Builders*

2. Kwaku visited some friends in Kumasi. He asked the people in the village where they work. Use the information he got to complete Kwaku's chart.

   - Five people work for the government.
   - Nine people work on farms.
   - Two people build things.

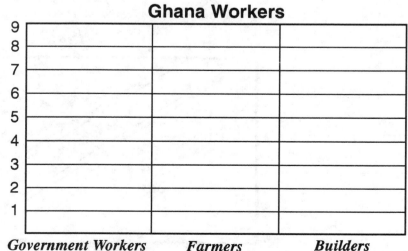

Ghana Workers

Government Workers   *Farmers*   *Builders*

Nessa's Fish: Summing It Up

Nessa's Fish is the story of an Inuit (Eskimo) girl and her grandmother who walk a great distance from their autumn camp to find a good salmon fishing area. Once there, they catch more fish than they are able to carry. Simultaneously, the grandmother becomes very ill and must rest. Nessa watches over her grandmother and the fish. When a fox, wolves, and a bear each approach to take the fish and possibly harm Nessa and her grandmother, Nessa frightens them away. She shows herself to be both quick-witted and brave. Nessa's family is proud of her when they eventually arrive to help her grandmother and Nessa home.

Getting to Know the Author

Nancy Luenn grew up in Los Angeles, California. She was the oldest child in a family of six brothers and sisters. Her mother spent a great deal of time reading to her large family. The entire family would sometimes go to the library and check out up to sixty books at once. Ms. Luenn's family did not own a television or have a fancy backyard, so the children created fun by using their imaginations. Ms. Luenn loved to listen to stories, especially fantasies. She also enjoyed digging in her backyard and creating imaginary worlds.

Ms. Luenn writes because she enjoys creating worlds that seem real. The ideas for her books come from her love of nature, her interest in animals, and her fascination with legends and fantasies. She attended Evergreen State College in Olympia, Washington, and she began writing children's books while she was still in college. She is the author of *Unicorn Crossing, Arctic Unicorn,* and *The Ugly Princess.*

Ms. Luenn now lives in Seattle, Washington. She loves the outdoors. Some of her hobbies include skiing, canoeing, and gardening. She is involved with many organizations that are concerned with protecting and saving the earth.

Getting to Know the Illustrator

Neil Waldman is the illustrator for *Nessa's Fish,* one of the first story books that he has ever illustrated. His background is primarily in illustrations for magazines and print advertisements. He has designed postage stamps for ten different countries, and he is also well known for his book covers and record album covers.

Mr. Waldman was born in New York City. As a child, he enjoyed art so much that he decided to one day make his living as an artist. After graduating from the Rochester Institute of Technology, he began his career as an illustrator. He now lives in White Plains, New York, with his wife and two children.

Getting Started

1. **History of the Inuit:** Share the following information with the students.

The Inuit are now known throughout the world as *Eskimos*. This name was given to them by the Cree Indians. Eskimo means "people who eat raw fish." Inuit means "the people."

Ten thousand years following the Ice Age, a group of hunters wandered into what is now known as the arctic region. Today we know this area as Greenland, Northern Canada, Alaska, and parts of Russia. The hunters came from Asia. Because the land had warmed considerably, the hunters were successful in catching game. As they followed the animals, they spread from Alaska to Greenland.

The people of the arctic survived by hunting and trapping game. In the beginning, they hunted the mammoth and then the caribou and sea mammals. Their lives revolved around survival in the cold arctic region. Food, clothing, shelter, and transportation would not have been possible without the animals the Inuit hunted. The Inuit were able to use practically every part of the animals they hunted.

Interestingly, not all Inuit lived in igloos. In fact, these were only one type of winter home. Some lived in sod houses during the winter months. Tents were used during the warmer months of the year.

Half of the year was spent preparing for the long winter. Large extended families banded together. The men hunted, and the women sewed and preserved the food that was caught. The people worked together and shared their food. At times during the spring and summer, small groups would leave the family to hunt. When it was time to hunt whales or walruses, the people would work together and share the fruits of their labor.

The Inuit were an ingenious group of people. They knew how to dress for the bitter cold. They designed waterproof suits to wear in a kayak or *umiak*. Travel was made easier by placing moss on the bottoms of their boots. They even made boots for their dogs to wear when pulling the sleds. Some sleds made from dried salmon could be eaten in an emergency. These survivalists had learned how to make it in the harshest conditions.

Today the Inuit are still strong survivors. They combine their old ways with the new. Like many other Native American people, they struggle to keep their beliefs, traditions, and values alive in each generation.

Getting Started *(cont.)*

2. **Before the Book:** Ask the students what they imagine the arctic to be like. Listen to their ideas. Then, have the students brainstorm for all the animals they think might live in the arctic. Tell them that they are going to listen to the story of a brave girl who lives there and who will have to frighten away some arctic animals. Have them predict how she will do this.

3. **Acting:** After reading, ask the students to recall the animals that Nessa scares away and how she does so. Ask them to explain how each situation involves acting.

   Now, have the students partner up. One child in each pair will play Nessa, and the other will be an animal. Call out the name of one animal (fox, wolf, or bear). The child in each team who is pretending to be the animal will act the way the animal acts in the story. The child pretending to be Nessa will scare the animal away just as Nessa does. After each child has acted out a role, have the students switch roles. This time call out a different animal.

4. **Go Away!:** After the acting game is over, have the students complete page 114. This sheet will check their understanding of the story and the sequence of events.

5. **I Can Be Scary:** Ask the students if they have ever played a trick on a family member or friend, or if they have ever tried to scare somebody in a harmless way (for example, hiding in a closet or sneaking up behind a person and yelling, "Boo!"). Allow the students to share some of these silly things they have done. On the board, make a list of what they have done.

On page 115, the students will have an opportunity to describe how they would frighten away animals or people. Make sure they know that they are to think of things that are funny but not dangerous.

An ethical discussion of "scaring others" might be worthwhile here. If others are scared by you, does that make you braver, stronger, or better than they are?

Name_____

Go Away!

Directions: Read each sentence. Number the sentences in the order that they happened. Then, cut out and glue each picture next to the sentence that it matches.

Nessa sings a silly song.

Nessa flaps her arms and shouts.

Nessa stands up as tall as she can and growls.

wolf

bear

fox

Name_____

I Can Be Scary

Directions: Read each partial sentence, and then decide what you would do to frighten away each animal or person.

1. I can scare my dog by

   _____

   _____

2. I can scare my sister by

   _____

   _____

3. I can scare my friend by

   _____

   _____

4. I can scare my cat by

   _____

   _____

5. I can scare a monster by

   _____

   _____

6. **Challenge:** Write a story about a time when somebody scared you.

   _____

   _____

   _____

   _____

   _____

   _____

   _____

   _____

   _____

People Are People

1. **Nessa's Feelings:** Read *Nessa's Fish* once more, but before doing so, ask the students to think about Nessa's feelings as they listen to the story. They will have to assume things about her feelings where they are not stated. Now, reread the story.

   Discuss the feelings Nessa has, or may have had, through each part of the story. Make a word web on the board (with "Nessa's Feelings" in the center) that lists all her feelings. Ask students to share examples of when they may have felt just as Nessa does.

2. **Feelings Journal:** It is amazing how often feelings can change. Students should have seen that Nessa has many feelings through the course of the story. The students themselves experience a variety of feelings through the course of their days. To illustrate this, each student can make and complete a feelings journal.

   To make the journal, each student will need at least ten pieces of paper and one piece of construction paper (all the same size). Stack the papers, placing the construction paper on the bottom. Fold the papers in half so that the construction paper is now on the bottom and the top. Staple down the side to make a journal. On the cover, each student can write his or her name and the word *private*.

   Next, brainstorm for a list of feelings. Write them on a piece of chart paper and keep them posted in the classroom.

   Have the students use their journals throughout an entire day of school. Each time they are aware of a feeling, or each time you ask them how they are feeling (perhaps at regular intervals or when a timer goes off), they should write the feeling or feelings and the experience down in their journals.

   After they have used their journals for an entire day, have them read over what they wrote. Ask them to list the number of feelings they had and to tally how many times they felt each way. Use the information from each student to make a class feelings chart. Discuss which feelings were the most "popular." Try the journals again another day and see if there is a difference.

Socializing Skills Project: Bravery

The purpose of this unit is to define bravery and to teach the students the difference between bravery and foolishness. The students will have an opportunity to determine some of their natural and instinctive bravery as well as to explore why they are now brave enough to do some things that they used to be afraid to do.

1. **Discussion of Bravery:** Begin the lesson by asking the students what they think it means to be brave. After listening to their suggestions, ask them if they think Nessa is brave. Then, explain that in order to be brave you must do the following:

   A. **Believe in yourself.**

   B. **Think before you act.**

   C. **Try new things.**

   D. **Know the difference between foolishness and bravery.**

   Discuss these four points as they relate to Nessa. You might consider the following in your discussion:

   Nessa never gives up or doubts her ability to frighten away the animals.

   She always tries to recall what other people have told her about each animal.

   She is ready to try new things, like talking to wolves and singing a silly song to a bear.

   She knows it would be foolish to run from the bear or to hit the wolves, for she or her grandmother might then have been seriously hurt.

2. **Foolish or Brave?:** Tell the students that the class is going to write a definition for *foolish*. Have them look in their dictionaries to see how the definition is written. Discuss how the words are printed with spaces between each syllable. Look at several words to demonstrate that sometimes a word has more than one meaning. In some dictionaries the word will be used in a sentence. Brainstorm different meanings for the word *foolish,* and then list them on the board. Have each student pick out three meanings that he/she likes the most. On a piece of paper, each student will write the word and the three meanings selected. Then he/she will create a sentence (using the word) for each meaning.

   Following this activity, ask the students if they have ever done something foolish because they were dared to do it or because somebody called them "chicken." Explain that some people confuse being brave with being foolish. Have the students compare their definitions of *foolish* with the definition that you gave them for *brave.* Encourage them to find the ways in which the two words are opposite to one another. For example, when a person is brave, he/she thinks about something before doing it. When a person is foolish, he/she acts without thinking.

   Pass out and complete page 119. This page will give the students an opportunity to distinguish between the two words.

Socializing Skills Project: Bravery *(cont.)*

3. **Being Brave Is...:** Invite the students to complete the following open-ended sentence: "Being brave is...." Above the sentence, the students can draw a picture to illustrate it. Make a class big book on bravery by stapling all the papers together or mounting each page on colorful construction paper and hooking them together with yarn or metal rings.

4. **Brave Enough:** Share with the class a time when you were not brave. Discuss how all people experience times when they are afraid to do something. It is natural to be afraid. As we grow older, we usually learn more about our fears, and eventually we build up the courage to be brave. Ask the students how many of them used to be afraid to come to school or to spend the night away from their parents. Encourage them to think of other things that they used to be afraid to do. List their suggestions on the board. Reassure them that it is okay to be afraid to do certain things. Also, point out that they now do many things that they once were afraid to do. Then, have the students complete page 120. This page will give them an opportunity to share something that they are now brave enough to do, although they did not used to be. When they draw the pictures to go with each sentence, remind them to draw the way they looked when they were afraid, keeping in mind that they were probably much younger then, too.

5. **Bravery Bulletin Boards:** Refer to page 121 for several techniques and clever bulletin board displays about bravery.

6. **Award of Bravery:** After reviewing the students' work, give each child an Award of Bravery (page 122). The award might mention the event that the child wrote about on page 120.

Name_____

Foolish or Brave?

Directions: Read each sentence. Decide if the act is a foolish or brave one.
Circle your choice.

1. Riding a bicycle without training wheels   **Foolish**   **Brave**

2. Running across a busy street   **Foolish**   **Brave**

3. Sleeping in a dark room   **Foolish**   **Brave**

4. Diving off a diving board   **Foolish**   **Brave**

5. Teasing a big dog   **Foolish**   **Brave**

6. Riding on a big rollercoaster   **Foolish**   **Brave**

7. Jumping out of a tree   **Foolish**   **Brave**

8. Hiding from your parents in the mall   **Foolish**   **Brave**

9. Picking flowers from a stranger's garden   **Foolish**   **Brave**

10. Going to a new school   **Foolish**   **Brave**

Name_____

Brave Enough

Directions: Read each partial sentence below, and then fill in the blanks. Draw yourself doing the brave actions.

1. At home, I used to be afraid to _____. Now I am brave enough to _____.

2. At school, I used to be afraid to _____. Now I am brave enough to _____.

3. In my neighborhood, I used to be afraid to _____. Now I am brave enough to _____.

4. On the playground, I used to be afraid to _____. Now I am brave enough to _____.

Bravery Bulletin Boards

1. **Heroes at Large:** Construct a bulletin board that displays pictures and articles about people who have done brave things. As a homework assignment, the students can look through newspapers or magazines with their parents to find these pictures and articles. As a corresponding activity, students can act out the articles for the class. If any of the students have done brave acts that saved other people from harm, allow them to write a news story about the event. Include these papers on the bulletin board.

2. **A Brave Class:** Have the students illustrate themselves doing something they feel is brave (something they have actually done). This should be an act in which the individual student takes pride. For example, Stephanie might draw herself sleeping in the dark, and Mark may illustrate the time he warned a walking man just before he got hit by a bicyclist. Display these illustrations on a bulletin board. As a caption for each, have the students write a sentence about the brave act depicted.

3. **Brave or Foolish?:** Illustrate the foolish and brave acts from page 119 as well as any others that the class can think of and would like to include. Divide a bulletin board with a line down the middle. At the top of the left side, write "Brave." At the top of the right side, write "Foolish." Place the illustrations on their appropriate side. You might also cut pictures from magazines and newspapers, and then ask the class whether each act depicted is brave or foolish. Once again, place the pictures on their appropriate sides.

Award of Bravery

This Award of Bravery is presented to _____ .

for showing bravery by _____

Be it known that from this date, _____ ,

is recognized as a brave citizen of _____

School.

Teacher

Principal

Getting from Here to There

1. **The Poles:** Show the students a globe and ask them to describe everything they notice about it (the shape, the bodies of land and water, the equator, etc.). Make sure the students realize that the globe is slightly tilted to one side. Explain that the earth itself tilts to one side. The tilt of the earth gives us our seasons.

   Point out the North and South Poles. When the North Pole is slanted toward the sun, it is summer there. When the North Pole is slanted away from the sun, it is winter there. During winter, it takes longer for the sun's rays to reach the North Pole, and this is why it is colder. When the North Pole is slanted away from the sun, the South Pole is slanted toward the sun. When the North Pole is slanted toward the sun, the South Pole is slanted away from the sun. This will create opposite seasons at the poles, and likewise it will create varied seasons around the world.

   Have the students complete page 125. This page will help the students identify the polar regions.

2. **Seasons in the Arctic:** Since the tilt of the earth is responsible for the seasons, the seasons are quite different in the polar regions. Use the following information to help your students complete page 126.

   Winter at the North Pole can last up to six months. It usually begins in early October and ends in March. The temperature remains below the freezing point for months. Not a lot of snow falls on the land, but what does come down is swept into huge snowdrifts.

   Blizzards of blowing snow are quite common. Daylight is present for only a few hours. In the far northern reaches, it also remains dark from late October until February. Many people live in snowhouses during these winter months. (See page 128 for more information about snowhouses.)

   Spring usually lasts from late March until June. During March and April, it continues to snow. However, the temperature begins to warm and the days grow longer. The people move out of their snowhouses during this season. They set up tents near the water.

   Summer will last for only a few weeks in July and August. The sun is out for most of the day. This is why the arctic is sometimes called the Land of the Midnight Sun. During this time, the tundra becomes very wet from the melting snow. The water from the snow does not seep into the ground because of the permafrost (a layer of earth just below the surface that is permanently frozen); therefore, flooding is common during this time. Despite the floods, flowers begin to bloom and plants such as lichens can be seen growing everywhere. The people continue to live in tents, but they will travel far and wide to go to the summer trading festivals. They are careful during the summer to stock up on items they will need during the winter.

Getting from Here to There *(cont.)*

Autumn begins in September and ends by October. Light snow begins to fall during this season. The days grow shorter and colder. Birds begin to fly south, and the people are busy hunting caribou and musk oxen. The meat from these animals will be dried and stored for use during the winter. The people gradually begin to move from their summer tents into their winter homes. By October, the Inuit must be prepared to survive the long winter.

Page 126 will allow the students to explore the seasons in the arctic and the seasons in their own area.

3. **Inuit Months:** Like many ancient civilizations, the Inuit determine their months according to the phases of the moon. Some of the months are named for what is happening in nature to the animals. Other names relate to chores undertaken by the people. December, January, and February are named according to the weather and astronomy. Below are the Inuit meanings for the twelve months of the calendar.

> **January:** Moon of the returning sun
> **February:** Coldest moon
> **March:** Moon for bleaching skins
> **April:** Moon for beginning whaling
> **May:** Moon when rivers flow
> **June:** Moon when animals give birth
> **July:** Moon when birds raise their young
> **August:** Moon when birds molt
> **September:** Moon when birds fly south
> **October:** Moon when caribou rut
> **November:** Moon of the setting sun
> **December:** Moon with no sun

Ask your students to come up with new names for the months. The names should reflect changes in nature or in the weather patterns of your community. Names can also refer to things that people do during certain months. For example: September can be "Moon when children return to school" or April can be "Moon when umbrellas are used."

4. **Complete the Map:** Look through the illustrations in *Nessa's Fish*. Have the students identify the various forms of plant and animal life as well as the geographical features that they see.

Explain to the students that Nessa lives on a tundra. The ground of a tundra is frozen for most of the year. One foot below the top soil is a layer of earth known as *permafrost*. This part of the ground is permanently frozen. It does not snow a great deal on the tundra, but it is bitterly cold. The winds are very strong, and they blow the snow into huge snowdrifts. There are no trees on the tundra because it is so cold. Plants that grow there do not grow very tall. Small shrubs such as heather, lichen, and reindeer moss grow across the tundra. These plants must survive the icy, long winters. Caribou, lemmings, and musk oxen (as well as the bears, wolves, and foxes of the story) are some animals that live on the tundra. These animals survive by feeding on moss and grass.

Discuss all these elements of the tundra, and then have the students complete the map on page 127.

Name_____

The Poles

Directions: Follow the directions for each item below.

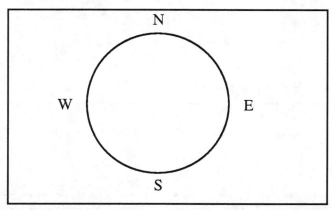

1. This is the earth. Draw a patch of ice where the North Pole is.

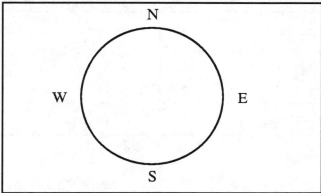

2. This is the earth. Draw a patch of ice where the South Pole is.

3. When it is winter at the North Pole, the North Pole is slanted away from the sun. Draw the sun.

4. When it is summer at the North Pole, the North Pole is slanted toward the sun. Draw the sun.

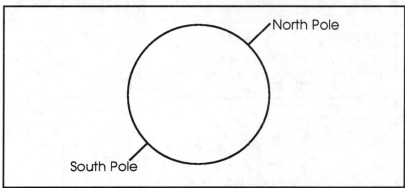

Name_____

Seasons in the Arctic and at Home

Directions: Use the following symbols to fill in the calendars.

Winter  **Spring** **Summer** **Fall**

The Seasons in the Arctic

January	February	March	April

May	June	July	August

September	October	November	December

The Seasons at Home

January	February	March	April

May	June	July	August

September	October	November	December

Name_____

Complete the Map

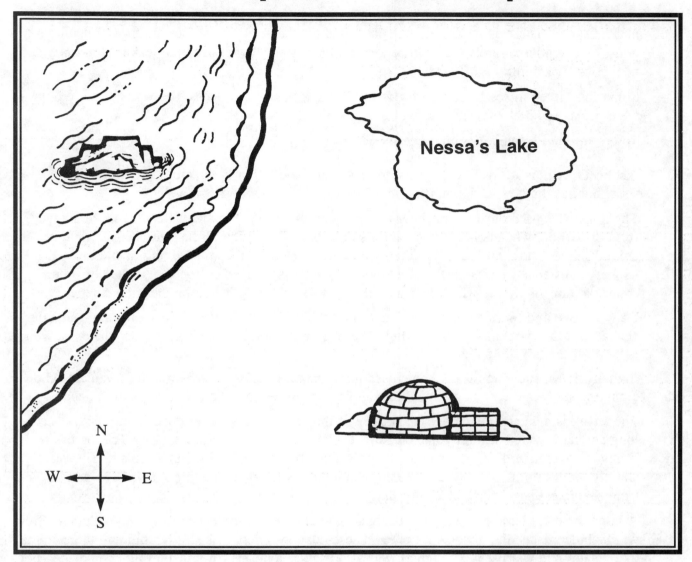

Directions: Follow the directions given in each step below. Copy the symbols provided.

1. Cover the ground with permafrost.
2. Place a polar bear cave to the right of Nessa's lake.
3. Add a polar bear inside the cave.
4. Draw two seals in the Arctic Ocean.
5. Place one bush on each side of Nessa's igloo.
6. Add five salmon in the lake.
7. Draw a snowdrift in the bottom right corner.

Experiencing the Culture

1. **Arctic Homes:** In the winter months, some Inuit used to live in igloos built from hard blocks of packed snow. These snowhouses sometimes had tunnels leading to other rooms or a neighbor's house. Snowhouses rarely lasted the entire winter. Once a home began to leak or get drafty, a new house was built.

   Some Inuit lived in sod houses with a frame of stones or whalebones. The walls of these homes were packed with earth. They lasted for a long time.

   Today, the Inuit usually live in modern houses.

2. **Arctic Transportation:** The principal modes of transportation in the arctic are dogsleds, snowmobiles, kayaks, and umiaks.

   The dogsled is used during the winter to travel across frozen land and water. The sled is made from driftwood, whalebone, caribou antlers, or ivory. The frame of the sled is covered with animal skins. The runners are prepared with a hot paste made from mud, moss, and turf. This slippery substance freezes quickly, and then hot water is sprayed on top of it. The hot water creates a thin film of ice which increases the sled's ability to glide along the snow and ice.

   Between two and fourteen dogs are used to pull the sled. The driver usually runs alongside the sled and calls out commands to the dogs. People rarely ride on the sleds because the extra weight is hard for the dogs to pull.

   In many areas, snowmobiles are now used more than dogsleds. These motorized vehicles glide along the snow and ice. Sometimes snowmobiles are used in the place of dogs to pull sleds.

   The kayak is made by attaching seal skin or caribou skin to a wood or bone frame. Kayaks are long and narrow and seat only one person. They are usually used for hunting. The top of the kayak is covered with skins, and there is only a small opening for the hunter to sit. The vessel silently moves through the water, guided by a hunter wearing a waterproof suit. The suit, made from seal intestines, keeps the hunter dry.

   A larger boat, called the umiak, was designed to hold many people. It is an open boat made from walrus hide attached to a wooden frame. These boats were once used when hunting large animals like whales and walruses. The umiak was also used as a means for transporting people and goods.

   Students can learn more about these forms of transportation by completing page 130. After completing the page, encourage the students to draw and cut out one of the modes of transportation used in the arctic. Collect their artwork and create a bulletin board that displays how each vehicle is used. Encourage the students to apply what they know about the geographical structure of the arctic when designing a background for the bulletin board.

3. **Inuit Games:** Page 131 offers several fun games for students to play while studying the Inuit culture.

4. **Inuit Language:** Page 132 introduces *Inuktitut,* the Inuit language.

Experiencing the Culture *(cont.)*

5. **Inuit Recipes:** The Inuit dried most of the meat they caught. They discovered that when dried, meat would store and transport better. During the long winter, their supply of dried meat was vital. They even sometimes used dried salmon to make sled runners. In life-threatening situations, the runners could be eaten.

   Page 133 offers some easy Inuit recipes to try and enjoy.

6. **Inuit Clothing:** Today, the Inuit often wear modern clothing. However, they once depended solely on animal skins and furs to clothe their bodies. Inside the igloo and during warm weather, they wore shorts made from foxskin. During the winter, each person wore two parkas, two pairs of pants, two sets of mittens, stockings, and boots known as *mukluks*. Next to the skin, the Inuit wore a furlined parka. The warmth of the fur next to the body helped to trap heat. Another parka was worn on top of the first parka. It had fur on the outside. The parkas had drawstrings at the wrists, waist, neck, and face. The mittens, worn with the fur against the skin, served a dual purpose. The outer pair could be taken off and used as a seat cushion if the Inuit had no shelter and needed to rest. Mukluks were made from fur and the bottoms were lined with moss. They kept the feet warm and dry. The moss prevented the feet from slipping on the ice. The mukluks were tightly fastened to the legs by tying a string around the top of the boot.

   A mitten pattern is provided on page 134 and mukluk directions on page 135. To make the mittens, each student will need four mitten patterns. Cut the patterns along the solid lines. Hold two mittens together and punch holes around all edges but the bottom. String the sides together with yarn. Glue a cotton trim to the opening of the mittens.

   A clothing puzzle can be found on page 136. Have the students compare the clothing that they wear to what the Inuit used to wear.

7. **Philosophy and the Snowy Owl:** The Inuit worshipped nature spirits who protected them. They felt that all people and animals had spirits. Certain spirits ruled over the land and the sea. The Inuit feared the spirits. They tried their best to please the spirits by obeying certain laws.

   The animals that were hunted were treated with respect. A ritual of offering fresh water to a dead seal was quite common. The people thanked the animal for giving its life so that the Inuit could sustain their own lives.

   The Inuit held a strong belief in Sedna, the mermaid. The legend of Sedna's life explains how an Inuit girl drowned in the water after her fingers were chopped. She began to live under the water with the animals and was the most powerful human spirit. It was believed that she determined a hunter's success.

   Okpik was the spirit owl. Its name means snowy owl. Okpik was a lucky charm for the Inuit, protecting all of nature in the north. Okpik was also the guardian of the polar bear and the geese. Much Inuit art depicts Okpik. To learn more about the snowy owl, complete page 137.

Name_____

Arctic Transportation

The *dogsled* was used to cross the snow and ice. The sled was made from wood or large bones. It was pulled by two to fourteen dogs. The sled carried tools and food. The driver of the sled rarely rode on it. Most of the time the driver ran along the side and guided the dogs.

The *snowmobile* has replaced the dogsled. It is powered by an engine. It can carry people, tools, and food. The driver always rides on the snowmobile, and more than one person can fit on one. Sometimes a snowmobile pulls a sled.

The *kayak* was a boat built for one. It was made from animal skins and wood. The kayak was used for hunting. The hunter would silently paddle through the water looking for seals.

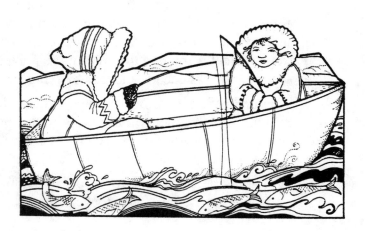

The *umiak* was a large boat. There was enough room for eight people to sit. Each person on the umiak would paddle. Sometimes several umiaks would work together to kill a whale and bring it to the shore. This boat was made from animal skins and wood.

Directions: After reading the information above, read each sentence below and decide which type of transportation is being described.

1. Only one person rides in this craft. _____

2. Eight people can ride in this craft. _____

3. Animals pull this craft. _____

4. This craft uses an engine. _____

5. Whales were hunted in this craft. _____

6. The driver does not sit in this craft. _____

7. This craft is paddled by only one person. _____

8. This craft has replaced the dogsled. _____

Inuit Games

1. **Ptarmigans and Ducks:** The game of tug-of-war has been played throughout the world. Here is the way the Inuit once played the game. Shortly before winter began, the people played "ptarmigans and ducks." (The ptarmigan is an arctic bird that endures the cold winters while the duck flies south.) All of the people in the village were divided into two groups. Those born in the winter were the ptarmigans. The rest (considered the people of summer) were the ducks. The two teams pulled a rope made from sealskin. If the ptarmigan team won, that meant the winter would be long and harsh. If the ducks won, the winter would not be so harsh.

   To play the game, divide the class according to birthdays. (Remember that winter in the arctic lasts from October through February.) Have the teams pull on a long jumping rope. Use masking tape to make a dividing line on the floor. The team of the first person to step on or across the line loses the match. This game is a lot of fun, so play the best of three before determining the winner.

2. **Cat's Cradle:** The Inuit once had to spend most of the long winter inside their homes. For entertainment, they sometimes played games with string. Today, we call these games *cat's cradle*. Cat's cradle is actually just one of hundreds of shapes that can be made from about two yards (1.8 meters) of thin, strong string or yarn. (A shorter length of string may be fine for children.) Check your library for some books that demonstrate the making of string shapes.

   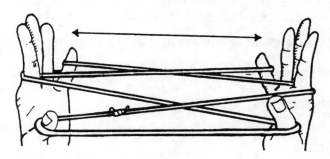

3. **Olympics:** An annual event for the Inuit is the Eskimo-Indian Olympics. This yearly event allows the Inuit to meet with old friends, share handmade crafts, display their art, watch dancers perform stories of their history, and participate in games which show their physical fitness. The event is held every year in Fairbanks, Alaska.

   The games are exciting. Some demonstrate endurance while others show strength and teamwork.

   Plan an Eskimo-Indian Olympic festival for your students. Display the mittens and mukluks they have made (pages 129 and 134-135), and award ribbons for creativity, beauty, and craftsmanship. Prepare the recipes (page 133) so the students can enjoy the food while they participate in the events. Provide children's books about the Inuit, and take some time to share the stories. Then, organize the games. You might include ptarmigan and ducks (described above), a hopping contest (wherein the athletes hop on one foot as a test of endurance—the one who hops the longest wins), and/or a kicking game (wherein the athletes kick a tetherball which is raised higher at every turn— the one able to kick the ball at its highest point wins).

Inuktitut: The Inuit Language

1. **About the Language:** Inuit translates to mean "the people." The Cree, Indian neighbors to the south of the Inuit, were the first to call the people *Eskimo*. Eskimo means "people who eat raw meat."

   The Inuit speak Inuktitut. Sentences in Inuktitut are made by adding to a root word, so that an entire sentence runs together as one word. For example, the sentence "He was not allowed to hunt caribou" would be written as "Hewasnotallowedtohuntcaribou." In Inuktitut, it is pronounced "tuttusiurqujaulaugituq."

   Until the nineteenth century, there was no writing system for Inuktitut. Missionaries helped to create a system that was based on Cree writing. This system is still used today.

2. **Making Inuktitut Sentences:** After discussing Inuktitut, have each student write three sentences about Nessa. Ask them to string the words of each sentence together. Now, have the students partner up, and then challenge each to guess what his/her partner has written. You may wish to model this activity first.

3. **Learning the Vocabulary:** Share the following Inuktitut words with the class:

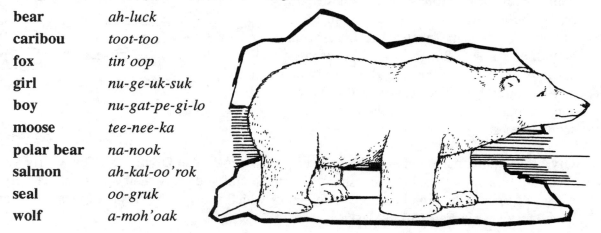

bear	*ah-luck*
caribou	*toot-too*
fox	*tin'oop*
girl	*nu-ge-uk-suk*
boy	*nu-gat-pe-gi-lo*
moose	*tee-nee-ka*
polar bear	*na-nook*
salmon	*ah-kal-oo'rok*
seal	*oo-gruk*
wolf	*a-moh'oak*

4. **Animal Books:** Have the students draw a picture of each animal named in the vocabulary list above. They can label them in both English and Inuktitut.

   To make a multicultural animal book, gather the names of these same animals in as many languages as you can. Use bilingual students, parents, school employees, and neighborhood friends as resources. The students can find the words in at least one other language for homework.

   Make the books in the same manner as the feelings journals (page 116), or make accordion books by folding long sheets of paper into an accordion fold. Draw a bear on the first page and write, "In Alaska, he is called *ah-luck*." On the second page, draw another bear and write, "In Mexico, he is called *oso*." (Or, use whatever language you have found.) Draw another bear on the third page and write, "But to me, he is a bear." If you have found more ways to say each animal name, use more paper.

Inuit Recipes

Salmon Salad

Ingredients:

- 1 quart (1 L) deli macaroni salad
- 4 3-ounce (90 g) cans salmon
- 1 box saltine crackers

Directions:

1. Combine the salmon and the macaroni salad in a medium-sized bowl.
2. Stir well.
3. Serve on crackers. Makes ten servings.

Agutuk Ice Cream

Ingredients:

- 2 egg whites
- ½ cup (125 mL) margarine or butter
- 1 3-ounce (90 g) can tuna or salmon
- 2 tablespoons (30 mL) vanilla extract
- brown sugar or honey to taste
- ½ cup (125 mL) berries (blueberries, cranberries, etc.)

Directions:

1. Beat egg whites until stiff.
2. Beat in butter.
3. Add vanilla and brown sugar.
4. Stir in salmon.
5. Add berries on top.
6. Eat and enjoy. Makes two servings.

Caribou Stew

Ingredients:

- 1 pound (500 g) beef (cubed)
- 2 ½ cups (625 mL) water
- 1 cup (250 mL) flour
- 1 medium onion (peeled and cubed)

Directions:

1. Simmer meat and onion in a saucepan until tender.
2. Combine water and flour. Stir until mixture is smooth.
3. Pour liquid over meat.
4. Stir over medium heat. Makes four servings.

Eskimo Icee

Ingredients:

- 2 cups (500 mL) clean snow
- ½ cup (125 mL) berries (blueberries, cranberries, etc.)
- sugar and honey to taste

Directions:

1. Stir all ingredients together in a bowl.
2. Eat and enjoy. Makes two servings.

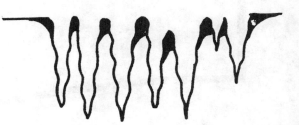

Make Your Own Mittens

See directions on page 129.

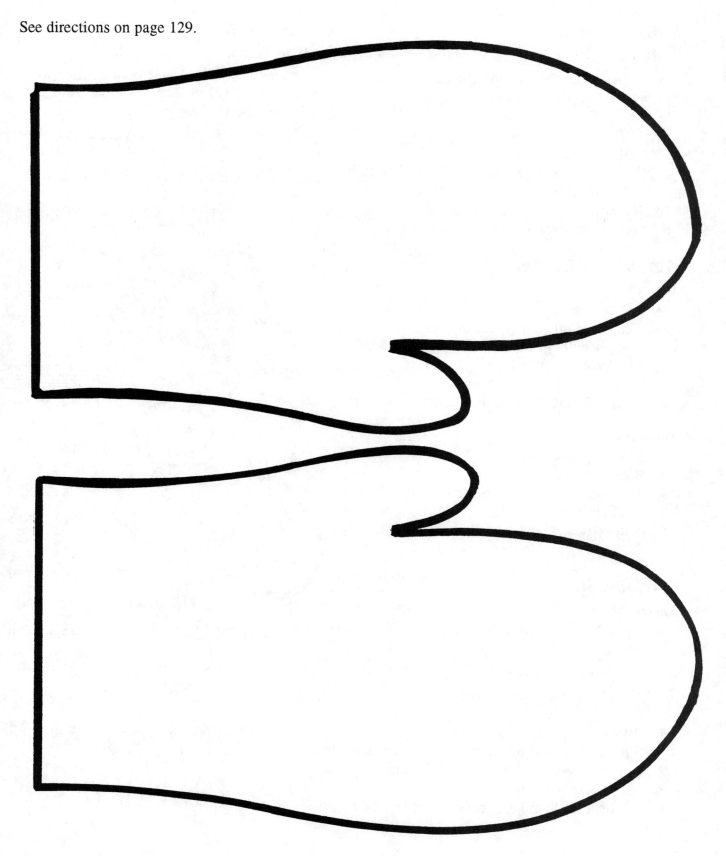

Make Your Own Mukluks

Materials:

- two medium-sized brown paper bags
- markers or crayons
- cotton balls
- twine
- glue

Directions:

1. Take off your shoe and make sure it fits inside the bag.

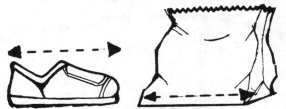

2. Decorate the bags by drawing designs and shapes.

3. Roll the tops down.

4. Glue cotton balls on the rolled part of each bag so that it looks like fur.

5. After the mukluks have dried, put them on. Tie them securely with twine under the rolled part.

Name_____

What Keeps You Warm?

Directions: Unscramble the words. Then use them in the crossword puzzle.

1. otosb _____
2. toca _____
3. tha _____
4. tsnmite _____

5. sptna _____
6. cafrs _____
7. kcsos _____

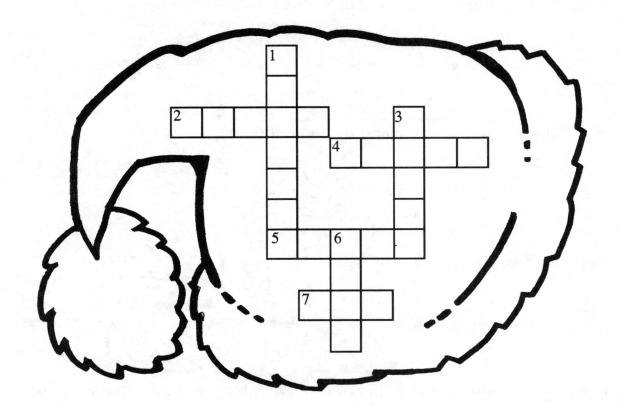

Across Clues

2. They keep your feet dry.

4. It keeps your neck warm.

5. These are worn right next to your feet.

7. This keeps your head warm.

Down Clues

1. They make your hands warm when holding snowballs.

3. Your legs will stay warm and dry when you wear these.

6. It keeps your body warm.

Name_____

The Snowy Owl

The snowy owl lives in the arctic. White feathers cover its body, legs, and feet. The feathers keep it warm. They also help the owl to blend with the snow and ice.

The snowy owl builds a nest near the water. The mother owl keeps the eggs warm, and the father owl hunts for food. Snowy owls like to eat lemmings. If there are not enough lemmings, the owls will fly south.

Directions: Read the paragraphs above, and then circle "true" or "false" next to each statement below.

1. The snowy owl lives in the arctic.   **true**   **false**

2. The snowy owl is brown.   **true**   **false**

3. The snowy owl hunts for seals.   **true**   **false**

4. The snowy owl blends with the snow.   **true**   **false**

5. The snowy owl makes a nest near water.   **true**   **false**

Community Ties

1. **What I Need to Know About Me**: In *Nessa's Fish*, Nessa is unable to go home because her grandmother is sick. She survives this emergency by remaining calm and by using her head.

   Discuss with the students what they may need to do in case of an emergency, especially if they should happen to get lost or separated from their caretakers. Use the following tips to teach your students what to do.

   The most important thing a child needs to know is the first and last name of his/her parent or guardian. Next, he/she needs to learn his/her phone number and address.

   Have the students take home page 139 for homework. After they have returned the completed page, have them work with a partner to memorize the information. Explain to the students that this is very important information for them to learn and to remember always.

2. **When You Are Lost:** In a large group discussion, invite the students to share experiences they have had when they were lost. Then, tell them they are going to learn some important rules to remember should they become lost.

   Tell the students that the most important thing is to remain calm. Ask them to consider what could have happened if Nessa had started crying very hard or if she had tried to run from the dangerous animals. Tell them that a calm person will be able to think clearly and remember the information he/she has memorized.

   The second rule is to stay in one general area. Do not start running around. Do not try to walk home or ask a stranger to take you home. If you are running around, it will be harder for your parents to find you, and it is not safe to walk up to a stranger or to get in his/her car.

   The third rule to follow is to make a phone call or an announcement. Go to a clerk, security guard, or someone in charge and ask that person to make an announcement. Or, ask to use the phone to call your parents. If you have remained calm, the person on the loud speaker will be able to say your parent's name and tell the parent where you are.

   After discussing the information, have the students complete page 140.

What I Need to Know About Me

My name is _____.

I live with _____.

              (first name)   *(last name)*

Here is a picture of us.

My phone number is _____.

My address is _____.

Here is a picture of my house.

Name_____

When You Are Lost

Directions: Review the three rules to remember if you are lost. Write the correct rule under each picture.

1.

_____

_____

2.

_____

_____

3.

_____

_____

Stay in one place.

Remain calm.

Ask someone in charge to make an announcement.

Bibliography

dePaola, Tomie. *The Legend of the Indian Paintbrush*. Macmillan, 1988

    Oliver Button Is a Sissy. Harper, 1979

Fradin, Dennis. *Hiawatha: Messenger of Peace*. Macmillan, 1992

Gryski, Camilla. *Many Stars & More String Games*. Morrow, 1985

Hoffman, Mary. *Amazing Grace*. Dial, 1991

Kipling, Rudyard. *The Jungle Book*. Puffin, 1988

Lubin, Leonard. *Aladdin & His Wonderful Lamp*. Delacorte, 1982

Luenn, Nancy. *Nessa's Fish*. Atheneum, 1990

Mattox, Cheryl Warren, ed. *Shake It to the One That You Love the Best: Play Songs and Lullabies from Black Musical Traditions*. Warren-Mattox Productions, 1989 (Call the publisher at 415-223-7089. Write: 3817 San Pablo Dam Road #336, El Sobrante, CA 94803.)

McDermott, Gerald. *Anansi the Spider: A Tale from the Ashanti*. Henry Holt & Company, 1972

Williams, Brian. *Joan of Arc*. Marshall Cavendish, 1989

World Around Songs. *East West Songs*. 5790 Highway 80 S., Burnsville, NC 28714

Yashima, Taro. *Crow Boy*. Viking, 1955

Zolotow, Charlotte. *William's Doll*. HarperCollins, 1972

Answer Key

Page 10: Chibi and You

Me: Answers will vary.
Chibi: Feels bored at school; Walks to school; Brings lunch to school; Has perfect attendance; Listens to the teacher; Is helpful at home; Understands nature.

Page 18: L.A.'s Little Tokyo

1. three
2. yes
3. clothing store
4. two
5. Central Avenue

Page 19: Japan and the U.S.A.

1. plane; boat
2. west
3. Pacific Ocean
4. islands
5. east
6. Sea of Japan

Page 20: Japanese Exports

1. cars
2. VCR's
3. auto parts

Page 21: Finding America in Japan

baseball; rock and roll; blue jeans; tennis shoes; fast food restaurant; soft drink; western clothes; movie theater; western movie

Page 25: Kanji

1. person
2. mountain
3. sun
4. ear
5. mouth
6. moon

Page 36: Profile on Kristi Yamaguchi

1. six
2. gold
3. Japanese

Page 37: Kristi Crossword

Down

1. Kristi
2. medal
3. practiced
4. Olympics
5. brother

Across

6. ice
7. skater
8. sport
9. sister
10. dentist

Page 38: Map Kristi's Day

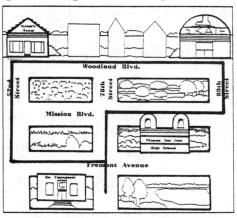

Page 39: Whose Shoe?   Page 44: I Can't/I Can

zori = Crow Boy
tennis shoe = American child
ice skate = Kristi Yamaguchi

1. run
2. paint
3. warriors
4. gift

Page 47: Words That Won't Quit

try again; work harder; keep going; don't stop; just do it; stick with it

Page 50: A Guide to Making Promises

Rule: Never make a promise that you are not willing to keep.

1. A promise is doing what you said you would do.
2. A promise is giving what you said you would give.
1. Do I want to make this promise?
2. Can I really keep this promise?
1. trust
2. disappoint
3. count

Page 51: A Promise You Can Keep

Answers may vary.
Never make a promise you are not willing to keep.

Page 53: Buffalo Hunt

1. Lookout Hills and the buffalo herd
2. east
3. south
4. north
5. west

Page 54: A Moving Village

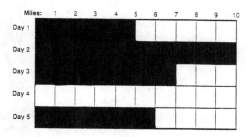

Answer Key *(cont.)*

Page 58: Living in a Tepee
1. false
2. true
3. true
4. false
5. true

Page 59: Reservation Life
1. B (31)
2. A (United States)
3. C (running water)
4. B (schools)
5. C (houses)

Page 60: Build a Home
The picture order is 3, 1, 2.

Page 61: Shared Values
A. tree, flower, buffalo, ocean
B. sun, clouds, rainbow, star, rain

Page 82: Real or Make-Believe?
1. make-believe
2. real
3. make-believe
4. real
5. real
6. make-believe
7. real
8. real
9. real
10. make-believe
11. real
12. make-believe
13. real
14. real
15. make-believe

Page 83: Great People from the Past
1. B
2. C
3. A
1. B
2. A
3. C

Page 85: Breaking Down Stereotypes
Stereotypes: 1, 2, 4, 6, 8, 9, and 10
Non-stereotypes: 3, 5, and 7

Page 86: Unscrambling Stereotypes
Note: Noun order in the sentences may vary.
1. Women and men can both be good drivers.
2. Boys and girls can take dance lessons.
3. Boys and girls can play baseball well.
4. Anybody can wear blue.
5. Girls and boys can cry when they are sad.
6. Anybody can play with cars, trucks, and dolls.
7. Boys and girls can wear pink.
8. Some men and women are good cooks.
9. Women and men can be doctors.
10. Anyone can become a secretary.

Page 93: Port of Spain, Trinidad
You arrive at Tragarete Road and Dundonald Street.

Page 97: Kente Cloth and Adinkra
1. F
2. T
3. T
4. F
5. F
1. T
2. F
3. T
4. F
5. T

Page 109: Flags
courage = red
purity = white
justice = blue
blood = red
minerals = gold
forests = green
earth = black
water = white
fire = red

Page 110: People at Work in Trinidad/Ghana

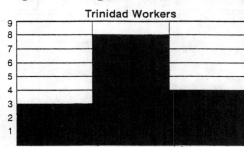
Trinidad Workers

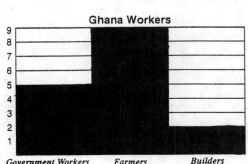
Ghana Workers

Answer Key *(cont.)*

Page 114: Go Away!

1. Nessa flaps her arms and shouts. (fox)
2. Nessa stands up as tall as she can and growls. (wolf)
3. Nessa sings a silly song. (bear)

Page 119: Foolish or Brave?

1. Brave
2. Foolish
3. Brave
4. Brave
5. Foolish
6. Brave
7. Foolish
8. Foolish
9. Foolish
10. Brave

Page 125: The Poles

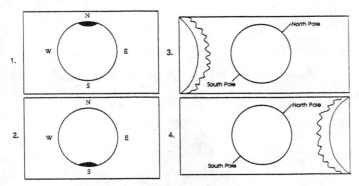

Page 126: Seasons in the Arctic

January	February	March	April
May	June	July	August
September	October	November	December

Page 130: Arctic Transportation

1. kayak
2. umiak
3. dogsled
4. snowmobile
5. umiak
6. dogsled
7. kayak
8. snowmobile

Page 136: What Keeps You Warm?

1. boots
2. coat
3. hat
4. mittens
5. pants
6. scarf
7. socks

Page 137: The Snowy Owl

1. true
2. false
3. false
4. true
5. true

Page 140: When You Are Lost

1. Remain calm.
2. Stay in one place.
3. Ask someone in charge to make an announcement.